David M. Childs/SOM

デイヴィッド・M・チャイルズ/ SOM

1976–1993

Architecture and Urbanism

September 1993 Special Issue
David M. Childs/SOM
1976–1993

1993年9月号別冊
デイヴィッド・M・チャイルズ/SOM
1976–1993

©1993 by a+u Publishing Co., Ltd.
Publisher:
Yoshio Yoshida
Editor:
Toshio Nakamura
Design Consultant:
Massimo Vignelli
Printed in Japan
Published by a+u Publishing Co., Ltd.
30-8, Yushima 2-chome, Bunkyo-ku,
Tokyo, 113, Japan
Phone: (03) 3816-2935
Fax: (03) 3816-2937
Distributor:
The Japan Architect Co., Ltd.
31-2, Yushima 2-chome, Bunkyo-ku,
Tokyo 113, Japan
Price Outside Japan:
¥4,800+¥1,500 (seamail postage)

ⓒa+u建築と都市
発行日：1993年9月20日
発行者：吉田義男
編集者：中村敏男
デザイン・コンサルタント：マッシモ・ヴィネリ
定価：3,800円(本体3,689円)/送料380円
振替：東京3-98119
発行所：株式会社エー・アンド・ユー
〒113 東京都文京区湯島2-30-8
電話：東京(03)3816-2935(代)
ファックス：(03)3816-2937
印刷所：大日本印刷株式会社
大取次：トーハン・日販・大阪屋・中央社・栗田出版・誠光堂
禁無断転載

Front cover: American Business Center at Checkpoint Charlie
Back cover: Deerfield Academy Natatorium

表紙：アメリカン・ビジネス・センター
裏表紙：ディアフィールド・アカデミィ屋内水泳場

編集者序文

この特集号はスキッドモア・オーウィングス・アンド・メリル建築事務所の代表であるデイヴィッド・チャイルズのワシントンやニューヨークなどにおける作品活動を紹介するものである。編集に当たって、中心的主題としたのは建築と都市の関係性である。個々の建築作品を単に紹介するだけではなく、それらが都市の文脈のなかでどのように位置しているか、どのような都市の条件のなかから作られたか、に留意している。建築と都市の関係は夙に言及されてきたがそれは単純一明快な関係ではない。試みに言うならば、建築は都市の可視的側面であり、都市は建築の不可視的側面である。こうした建築と都市の相互関係は最近になって認められたことではない。それは、ヴィトルヴィウス以来、すべての建築論がこの関係をめぐって展開されてきたと言っても過言ではない。アルベルティはきわめて明快に「住宅は小さな都市、都市は大きな住宅」と述べているではないか。しかし、この建築と都市の関係を実践的に言明した建築家は決して多くはない。その理由は、両者の関係が連続する領域の双極でありこの二極間に社会一文化の歴史的構造が介在しているからである。この複雑錯綜した構造的関係を空間的関係に翻訳するには果断な形態形成の還元作用が要求されるだろう。また勇敢な象徴機能の増幅作用が逆にその関係を解消しないともかぎらない。いずれにしても、建築と都市の相互関係の実際的な表明には個人的ないしは私的想像力とは別個の集団的ないしは公的想像力が要請されるこの両者の構造的関係と言い、その空間的関係への物理的転換と言い、連続する領域に独自の言語体系で直線的ないしは非可逆的に記述することは不可能であったから、それら関係性の認知は無論のこと、関係の正当性についてはほとんど無視されたままであった。歴史叙述には建築家の個人名は記載し易いが集団名は記載し難い。そして建築は個人的想像力の所産だとする神話は未だ生き続けている。それどころか、この神話は都市との相互関係の力学のなかで神学として位置づけられるまでに至った。このゴルディウスの結び目に例えられる関係性は多くの建築家を魅了してきたし、それを解放しようとする度毎に建築的英雄を生み出してきた。しかし、これは解決しても忽ち元に戻ってしまう結び目なのだ。元に戻るどころか、一層複雑度を増して立ち現れてくるのである。デイヴィッド・チャイルズの建築活動は建築的英雄を指向するものではない。むしろ、それを放棄することによって、つまり建築と都市の抜き差しならない関係性に平衡の力学を構築しようとしているのである。

Editor's Introduction

This special issue introduces the work and activities of David M. Childs, chairman of the Skidmore, Owings & Merrill (SOM) architectural firm, in Washington, New York, and elsewhere. The editorial theme focuses on the complex relations between architecture and the city. Rather than simply introducing a number of specific works, we have attended to the question of how each work is situated in the context of the city, how it was constructed within the conditions imposed by the city. The topic of architecture and the city is hardly a new one, but the relation it questions has never been either simple or self-evident. We might venture to epitomize the problem as follows: architecture is the visible aspect of the city; the city is the invisible aspect of architecture. The complex interactions between architecture and the city were recognized as early as Vitruvius, and it would not be an exaggeration to suggest that the entire discourse on architecture since then has revolved around these interactions. Alberti posed the problem very concisely when he wrote that a house is a small city, a city is a large house. However, the number of architects who have, through their practice, issued clear statements on the relation between architecture and the city is by no means large. The reason, surely, is that these are two poles of a continuum, mediated by the historical structures of society and culture. To translate these complex interactions into a spatial relation would call for a dramatic act of morphological reduction. And there is no assurance that a bold expansion of symbolic functions would not, after all, cancel out such an attempt at spatial translation. In any case, an actual expression of the interactions between architecture and the city would demand the work of a public imagination together with or along side the individual or private imagination. Because it has not been possible to give a linear and irreversible description of the structural relation between these poles, of their physical transposition into a set of spatial relations, in a language proper to their continuous field, the problem of apprehending these relations, even that of recognizing their authenticity, has been almost entirely neglected. Historical accounts favor the recording of the names of individual architects to the exclusion of collective names. And so the myth that architecture is a product of the individual imagination lives on. Indeed, such a myth has become the theology presiding over the dynamics of interaction between architecture and the city. Those dynamics have, like a Gordian knot, tantalized any number of architects, but each attempt to resolve the knot has only given rise to yet another generation of heroic individuals. Each time the knot seems to have been cut, it reappears, assuming ever more complex forms. The work of David M. Childs is not another pursuit of architectural heroism. On the contrary, by abandoning that pursuit, he has been able to construct a dynamics of equilibrium from the aporia posed by the relations between architecture and the city.

(Translated by Lewis Cook)

What is a *sine qua non* for an Architect?

What is a *sine qua non* for an architect?

My answer must be *balance*.

Architecture must always be appropriate while inventive;

rigorous but flexible;

playful yet disciplined.

And,

since the concept of *balance* demands that it also should have a counterpart,

it must be modified by *conscience*,

for this is the overriding force that informs design.

March 10, 1993

David M. Childs

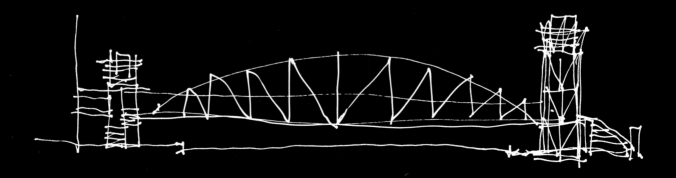

建築家としての必要十分条件とはいかなるものか？

建築家としての必要十分条件とはいかなるものか？

それはバランスをとることだと私は考える。なぜならば、

建築は常に創意に富むものである、と同時に

当面の目的にかなうものだからだ。

建築は常に精緻にして厳密である、しかし

柔軟にして自在でもあるからだ。

建築は常に楽しいものである、その上

規律正しいものでもあるからだ。

そうして、さらに

バランスが常に一対の相対するものから成り立つ以上、

バランスは良心の命ずるところに従うものでなければならない。なぜならば、

この良心こそデザインのすみずみに行きわたる大事な力であるからだ。

1993年 3月10日

デイヴィッド・M・チャイルズ

The following interview with David Childs was conducted by
Richard Sennett, University Professor of Humanities and Professor of
History and Sociology, at Professor Sennett's New York University
office. Professor Sennett explored Mr. Childs's evolution as a
designer—from his formative days working with Nathaniel Owings
on the Pennsylvania Avenue Plan for Washington, D.C. to his current
practice in New York City.
Mr. Childs became Chairman of Skidmore, Owings & Merrill in July
1991, and continues as well as Design Partner on his own
architectural and urban planning work. In the course of the
interview, Professor Sennett and Mr. Childs discussed four of Mr.
Childs's recent projects as they looked at drawings and photographs
of models. A brief summary of each of these projects is provided
below.

Columbus Center:
A mixed-use project of 2.5 million square feet, including office
space, luxury residential units, a multistory shopping and cinema
complex and parking, this project sits on Columbus Circle, the
southwest corner of Central Park. At this juncture four distinctive
city neighborhoods meet: Midtown Manhattan, the Clinton
neighborhood (formerly known as Hell's Kitchen), the Upper West
Side, and Central Park. The challenge was to knit these
neighborhoods together rather than to hold them apart.

Riverside South:
Throughout the major cities of the industrialized world, former

ard Sennett Interview with David Childs

次のインタヴューは、人文科学および歴史・社会学の教授であるリチャード・
セネットによって、彼の、ニューヨーク大学のオフィスで行なわれた。セネッ
ト教授はチャイルズ氏のデザイナーとしての経歴をよく研究しており、それは、
ワシントンDC、ペンシルヴェニア・アヴェニューでのナサニエル・オーウィ
ングスとの初期の作品から、ニューヨークでの最近の作品に至っている。
チャイルズ氏は1991年の7月にSOMの会長となりながら、建築と都市計画の分
野でのデザイン活動も続けている。インタヴューの中で二人はチャイルズ氏の
最近の四つの作品について、図面と模型写真を見ながらディスカッションした。
それぞれのプロジェクトの概要は以下の通りである。

コロンバス・センター：

23万2,000m²の複合施設であり、オフィス、豪華な住居施設、多層にわたるショ
ッピング街と映画館、そして駐車場からなる。敷地はセントラル・パークの南
西の角、コロンバス・サークル。ここは、ミッドタウン・マンハッタン、クリン
トン地区(以前はヘルズ・キッチンとして知られていた)、アッパー・ウェスト、
そしてセントラル・パークという四つの地区が出合う。このプロジェクトは、こ
れら四つの地区を分断するのではなく、ひとつに結ぶ試みがなされている。

リヴァーサイド・サウス：

工業化された世界の主だった都市を通して、初期に工業化された港湾地域は、
再開発の対象になりつつある。この、かつて市の操車場であった約31万m²の敷
地には1万2,000戸の住居地区が計画されつつある。この開発の中心的なプロジ

ndustrial lands at the water's edge are becoming available for
redevelopment. This 76-acre site, a former railyard for the city, will
become a new neighborhood for 12,000 residents. The centerpiece of
the neighborhood is a 21-acre riverside park. A project of this size is
unusual for Manhattan; because of its location on the edge of a
politically active and economically diverse district, it is also a highly
prominent site in the public eye.

Worldwide Plaza:

Another project unusual for its scope is Worldwide Plaza, a
mixed-use project that fills the complete block between 8th and 9th
Avenues and 49th and 50th Streets on the west side of Manhattan.
Although it is only two blocks from Rockefeller Center, this project
faced the challenge of creating a prestige commercial address in a
part of the city known primarily for its history as Hell's Kitchen, a
formerly tough and lower income neighborhood. The project includes
a 1.5 million square foot office tower, 661 residential units, and a
major plaza, below which are movie theaters.

Tribeca Bridge:

A project small by SOM standards but nonetheless most significant in
the city is Tribeca Bridge, a 250-foot span that has been designed to
provide safe passage for students, neighborhood residents, and other
pedestrians across 12th Avenue, the major north-south traffic spine at
the west edge of Manhattan. Given its location and visual
prominence, the bridge also serves as a gateway and an icon for
Lower Manhattan and Battery Park City.

1

2

チャード・セネット、デイヴィッド・チャイルズに聞く　　　浜田明彦訳

クトが、約8万5,000㎡のリヴァーサイド・パークである。敷地が政治的に影
力があり、経済的にも他と異なった地域に位置するため、この規模のプロジ
クトは、マンハッタンではきわめて稀であり、一般の人々の目からしても卓
した敷地である。

ールドワイド・プラザ:

の規模においてやはりきわだったもうひとつのプロジェクトが、ワールドワ
ド・プラザである。これはマンハッタンの西側の8番街・9番街から、49丁
、50丁目へ到るブロックすべてを覆う複合施設である。ロックフェラー・セ
ターからわずか2ブロックしか離れていないが、このプロジェクトは、以前
やっかいで低所得者層の地域、ヘルズ・キッチンとしてその歴史を知られて
た場所の一角に、高級商業施設をつくるという計画に挑んでいる。14万㎡の
フィス・タワー、661の住居ユニット、そしてその下層に映画館を収容する大
なプラザによって構成される。

3

ライベカ・ペデストリアン・ブリッジ

OMの規準からすると小さいが、それにもかかわらずこの街において最も重要
のがトライベカ・ブリッジである。これは、マンハッタンの西岸の主だった南
交通のスパインである12番街を横切る、学生・近隣住民・その他の歩行者の
めの、76mのスパンを有するブリッジである。そのロケーションといい、視
的な効果といい、このブリッジは、マンハッタン南地域とバッテリィ・パー
・シティのゲートウェイであり、象徴にもなっている。

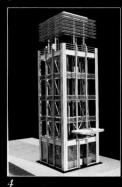

4

Sennett: I want to ask you about your design for the Columbus Center project. The original design by Moshe Safdie was unlike anything seen before in New York. Did you feel you were creating something more contextual, which is how your proposed project is often described?

Childs: I believe that design is at its best when we understand that it occurs both within and against constraints. These constraints are physical to a certain extent, but they are also cultural, societal, and political. When I began the design process for Columbus Center, I spent a good deal of time attempting to understand clearly the problems that were being expressed with the original design. I actually held up the new design for two months while I talked with a lot of New Yorkers who represented very different points of view. I wanted to design something that was not only appropriate to this city, but also tailored to this particular site, something that could not be transported to another site in New York or any other city in the world.

Sennett: In some sense, the ideal of context is also a terrible tyranny, isn't it? It's as though the city should be a seamless whole.

Childs: Context has nothing to do with the notion of seamlessness or repetition. Context is just as much about the program, about the users, and about people's reaction to the architecture, as it is about immediate physical surroundings. If you play the oboe in a jazz festival, you listen to what is going on around you and respond; you change tempo and key as appropriate. To ignore what is going on

5

1-*Columbus Center.*
   Photo by Betsy Feeley/SOM.
2-*Riverside South.*
   Photo by Bryan Nolan.
3-*Worldwide Plaza.*
   Photo by Jim Horner.
4-*Tribeca Pedestrian Bridge.*
   Photo by Stephen Weinryb/SOM.
5-*Columbus Center.*
   Sketch by David M. Childs.
   *(The following sketches are
   drawn by David M. Childs.)*
6-*Columbus Center.*

1-コロンバス・センター。
2-リヴァーサイド・サウス。
3-ワールドワイド・プラザ。
4-トライベカ・ペデストリアン・ブリッジ。
5-コロンバス・センター・スケッチ。
   (スケッチはデイヴィッド・チャイルズ
   による。以下のスケッチも同様。)
6-コロンバス・センター。

セネット: まずコロンバス・センター・プロジェクトのデザインについて質問したいと思います。モシェ・サフディによる当初のデザインは、ニューヨークにおいてかつて見たことのないようなものでした。あなたは、よりコンテクスチュアルなものをつくろうと考えていたのですか、あなたの作品がしばしば物語るような………。

チャイルズ: デザインがある制約の範囲内で、あるいは制約に対抗して生じるときこそ、最もよいデザインができるのではないかと考えています。これらの制約は、ある範囲において物理的なものであり、またやはり文化的、社会的、そして政治的なものでもあります。私がコロンバス・センターのデザインを始めたとき、当初のデザインのもつ様々な問題点をはっきり理解しようと、かなりの時間を費やしました。私はいろいろな観点をもつたくさんのニューヨーカーたちと話し合い、新しいデザインを実際2ヵ月間遅らせました。私はこの街にとって適切であるばかりでなく、この特別の敷地に完全にフィットするもの、ニューヨークや世界の他の都市の別の敷地にはそのまままってゆけない何かをデザインしたいと考えました。

セネット: ある意味において、コンテクストの考えというのは、おそろしく抑制的ではないですか、あたかも街全体が変化のない連続体であるような。

チャイルズ: コンテクストは変化のない連続体とか、繰り返しといった考えとは何ら関係がありません。コンテクストは、それがすぐそばの物理的な環境であるように、単にプログラムであり、建物の使い手とか人々の建築にたいするリアクションにすぎません。ジャズのフェスティヴァルでオーボエを吹くとき、周りの音楽的な進行に耳を傾けながら応えてゆく。テンポも、キィも適切に

around you is to produce cacophony.

Context is not about tyranny but about opening up opportunities. In fact, I believe that the least productive periods of art have occurred when the prevailing notion was "anything goes," when there was such a reaction against the tyrannical rules of a prevailing style that all constraining factors were dismissed, leaving nothing to push against.

Sennett: That expresses a psychoanalytic truth: a person who wipes the slate of memory clean is not free; one becomes free in dealing with the oppressive weight of memory, acknowledging and negotiating with the past. The "clean slate" is a horrific condition; Lacan called it the only truly terrifying act of repression.

Childs: Well said. My worst experience in designing without constraints was for a housing project in the Middle East. The site was absolutely open, surrounded by nothing but flat sand. There was a minimal program, and there were no budgetary limitations. With all these "freedoms," there was little to react to, and no clear goals except those I set myself.

In designing within the urban context, you have constraints such as budget, public policies and regulations, specified programs, and surrounding buildings—from which opportunities can be defined.

Sennett: One of the major design issues for Columbus Center was how the public space at the ground level would work with the round form created by the adjacent traffic circle. What was your conception?

Childs: Actually, one of the very few urban dictates given to the developers of the Columbus Center site was the mandate to reinforce the traffic circle in the form of a continuous streetwall at a minimum of 85 feet in height. This rule was specifically delineated in the urbanistic rules established for the competition.

I think it is a good rule for this site. "The Circle," as it is referred to on one of Olmsted's early plans for Central Park, has been so eroded over time that it badly needs reinforcement. The scale of the wall, the breadth of the sidewalk, the presence of the retail activity, and clear access to it—all those things are important to that site and that part of the city.

I had focused on this problem two years earlier when SOM was hired by the City of New York to conduct an urban design study of the circle itself. Our study revealed that over time, traffic patterns had created a "spaghetti" of movements, a dance of confusion within a serious, singular and understandable geometry. The traffic had driven people away. So our plan sought to reestablish the more important civic qualities of the space, to slow vehicles down to the benefit of the pedestrian.

What we tried to do with our plans for the traffic patterns themselves was to give some regular rhythm of trees and of pylons for information, while cleaning up traffic signage and other visual impediments. We allowed the desired movements toward the entrances to the subway station and preserved a variety of natural geometries of orderly movement around the spaces formed. So both our urban design plan for Columbus Circle and our architectural

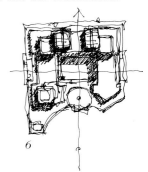

6

変えながら。周りで何が起こっているか無視することは突拍子もない音を出すようなものです。

コンテクストはおよそ抑制的なものではなく、機会を与えてくれるものです。要するに、その時点での共通した考えが「何でもできる」とか、あるいはそのときのスタイルの支配的な規律にたいするリアクションがある、それが、あらゆる強制的な要素が消え失せて何にも強いられないというときに、芸術の最も沈滞した季節が訪れるのではないかと考えます。

セネット: それはまさに精神分析学的な真実です。記憶の断片をきれいに消してしまう人は自由ではありません。人は、圧倒的な記憶、知識の重みを抱え、過去と交渉しながら自由になるのです。「きれいに消してしまうのは」ぞっとする状況です。ラカンはそれを、唯一真に恐ろしい抑制行為と呼んでいます。

チャイルズ: さて、抑制のないデザインの中で、私の最悪の経験は、ミドル・イーストのハウジング・プロジェクトでした。敷地はただ平坦な砂地に囲まれて、まったくオープンでした。最低限のプログラムはありましたが、予算上の制限はまったくありません。こうしたすべての「自由さ」とともに、私の解決したもの以外にいかなるリアクションも、いかなる明快な目標もありませんでした。

都市のコンテクストの中でのデザインにおいて、予算、公共の理念と法則、特別のプログラム、そして周辺をとりまく建物といった制約があるものです。そしてそこからチャンスが生まれるのです。

セネット: コロンバス・センターの最も大きなデザイン要素は、隣接する交差点と同様の円形の、地表レヴェルのパブリック・スペースがどのように機能するかということです。あなたの考え方はどういうものでしたか。

チャイルズ: 実際、コロンバス・センターのディヴェロッパーに与えられたきわめて少ない都市計画上の指示は、最低25.9mの高さで連続的な街の壁をつくりながらトラフィック・サークル（環状交差路）を補強するというものでした。これは、設計競技の中で都市計画上のルールとして特別に記述されていました。

私はこのルールはこの敷地にとってよいのではないかと考えました。「ザ・サークル」はオルムステッドのセントラル・パークの初期のプランに見られるように、あまりにも長い間侵蝕されてきたので、補強が深刻な問題となっていたのです。壁のスケール、歩道の幅、そして、今も続く商業活動とそこへのアクセス、こうしたすべてのことがこの敷地、この場所にとって重要なのです。

SOMが2年前に、このサークルの都市計画的検討をニューヨーク市から依頼されたとき、私は、この問題に焦点をあてました。私たちのスタディは、繰り返し生ずる交通パターンによって、「スパゲティ」のようなとりとめのない動き、深刻で単調で、理解できないような幾何学的な混乱を生じさせることを解明しました。交通は人々を遠ざけてしまいます。そこで、私たちの計画は、歩行者の利益となるように、自動車の速度を落として、より重要な都市空間の質をふたたび確立しようとすることでした。

私たちが、交通パターン計画として行なおうとしていたことは、交通標識やその他ヴィジュアルな障害物を一掃しながら、樹木や情報のための標塔に規則正しいリズムを与えることでした。地下鉄駅の入口へ集中する動線を許容し、形成された空間を取り巻く様々な秩序ある動きに伴う自然の幾何学を保護しまし

design for Columbus Center sought to reestablish the civic, public, and pedestrian character of this specific place.

Sennett: How are you putting some of these ideas into practice in the Riverside South project in which you are currently immersed? That is another project which has a history of vehement opposition.

Childs: Riverside South, which is a residential and open space project replacing derelict train yards and piers along the Hudson River in Manhattan, is particularly interesting because it is about completing a part of the city but at the same time reconnecting things that had been disconnected a long time ago. It has been the site of many unrealized initiatives, including a recent one that would have included the world's tallest building. Of course the surrounding neighborhood reacted vehemently against that proposal.

The current project, which extends over 13 city blocks, is a vestibule at the water's edge, running north and south. It represents the change from the natural scale along the river to the man-made scale of the city. It will include the largest new waterfront park to be built in Manhattan in our lifetime.

Within the site boundaries are many opportunities to address urban issues such as how buildings create pleasant street settings, how neighborhood-serving stores can enliven streets and make urban life more pleasant, and how whole communities that have not had access to the water's edge will now get there. Beyond its boundaries, though, the project will also have a profound effect on the way the neighborhood is used and enjoyed, and, because of that fact, much of the design attention has been given to the way this new neighborhood will relate to and extend the existing city.

Although the project will be built out over twenty years, its framework is being established now through an extended process of public review and approval. Design guidelines for individual buildings and open spaces are being developed as part of the master planning process. The challenge is to write these guidelines so they allow for conditions that cannot be predicted today. We must determine where to be restrictive and where to be relaxed so that we encourage a diversity of architectural expression, reflective of the rich variety of buildings that make up New York.

Sennett: To develop Riverside South in a way that knits it into the city, its real axis must be east-west rather than north-south. However, adjacent to the site's inland edge are a group of existing buildings that appear to constitute an impenetrable wall. How do you propose knitting the Riverside South project into this urban fabric?

Childs: That inland edge represents a great challenge for the Riverside South project, because its dimensions threaten the connectivity that is an essential characteristic of vital urban neighborhoods. The existing development you mentioned is made up of a series of large, impersonal, slab-buildings on sites created without reference to the scaling device of the New York City grid. Windswept and unfriendly, they destroy the scale and character that make this city liveable.

Rather than continuing such expression of scale, the new buildings

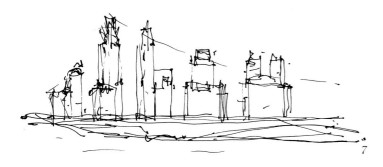

7

た。その結果、コロンバス・サークルにたいする私たちの都市計画デザインと、コロンバス・センターの建築デザインの両者は、この特種な敷地にたいする街の、公共の、そして歩行者の性格をふたたび確立しようとしたのです。

セネット： こういった考え方は、現在深く関わっているリヴァーサイド・サウス・プロジェクトにおいて、どのように表われてきていますか。それは激しい反対運動の歴史をもつプロジェクトであるわけですが。

チャイルズ： リヴァーサイド・サウスは、放棄された操車場と桟橋をマンハッタンのハドソン川に移しかえて、住居施設とオープン・スペースをつくり出すプロジェクトですが、長い間つながりのなかった地域を連結させると同時に都市の一部を形成するという意味で、大変興味あるものです。それは実現はしなかったけれども、たくさんの試みがなされた敷地であり、たとえば世界で一番高いビルという構想も含まれています。

もちろん近隣の住民はその提案にたいし、激しい抵抗を示しました。

この最新のプロジェクトは、南北に走る水辺の玄関であり、13以上のブロックにまたがっています。それは川に沿った自然のスケールから、街という人間の構築物のスケールへの変化を表わします。それは私たちの生涯において最も大きい、マンハッタンのウォーターフロント・パークも含んでいます。

敷地の境界には、いかに建物が快適な街路を創造できるか、いかに住民のための店舗が街路を活気づかせ都市生活を楽しくするか、今まで水辺へのアクセスができなかったコミュニティがいかにアクセスできるかといった都市計画上のアイデアを表現する機会に満ち溢れています。敷地の境界の外においてもこのプロジェクトは、近隣の人々が使い、楽しんでゆく方法でかなりの影響を与え

ることになるでしょうし、だからこそ様々なデザインに注意を払って、新しい住民も既存の市街に足をのばしながら関わってゆけるようにしました。

このプロジェクトは今後20年以上にわたって建設されてゆきますが、その骨格は、一般の人々の再検討や承認といったプロセスを経て、すでにできあがりました。それぞれ個別の建物やオープン・スペースのためのデザインのガイドインはマスタープランの一貫として確立されています。今日では予測できないような条件を許容するガイドラインをつくることはひとつの挑戦でした。私たちは、建築の表現に変化をつけさせ、ニューヨークの街を形づくる様々な豊かな多様性を反映させるように、どこに制限を設け、どこに設けないかを決定しなければなりません。

セネット： リヴァーサイド・サウスを町になじませるためには、その本当の軸は南北よりもむしろ東西にとる必要があります。しかしながら、敷地の周辺には、入り込めない壁を構成する既存の一群のビルがあります。あなたは、リヴァーサイド・サウスのプロジェクトをいかに街の中になじませるかについて、どのような提案を行ないましたか。

チャイルズ： 敷地の境界はリヴァーサイド・プロジェクトにとってきわめて挑戦的な課題です。なぜならば、そのスケールは、活気のある近隣地域のための本質的な性格である連結性をおびやかすからです。あなたのおっしゃったこれまでの開発は、ニューヨークのグリッドにスケールを合せずにつくられた、巨大で無人格で箱のような建物によって構成されています。吹きさらしで愛想がなく、街を活気づける性格とスケールを破壊するものです。

そのようなスケールの表現を続けるのではなく、リヴァーサイド・サウスでの

reated by Riverside South function like the bark of a tree—healing
he wound from behind and reestablishing a familiar pattern of
rowth as the city extends toward the river. Even though the grid
annot go all the way through because it is blocked by the existing
lab-buildings, it can reassert itself in a kind of "healing over," at the
ity's final edge.

ennett: So somehow life will take care of the wall?

Childs: Yes. Cities are not unlike the human body; they adapt; they
egenerate; they restore themselves. And those of us in the business
f treating cities are not unlike the surgeons who sometimes can
itch with enough precision that, over time, the scar will become
nvisible.

ennett: What strikes me about both the Columbus Center and
Riverside South projects is their suggestion that you as an architect
hink differently than architects of the last ten years, much more
bout social orientation and urban surroundings. You seem to stand
utside the style wars of the 1980s.

Childs: I hope so, but today there is such manipulation of facades
or their own sake, without regard to the structure as a whole, that I
ometimes despair for the future of architecture. I hope there will be
 return to the seriousness of architecture and a focus on
roblem-solving rather than fashion.

oing further back in history, many architects of the International
chool became fixed on the object. They ignored the larger context.
During my years of practice in SOM's Washington, D.C., office, I
learned many lessons about responding to urban surroundings.
Washington is a city with a tremendous sense of identity which
includes the powerful icons of the Federal City and Federal
architecture. It was there that I became enormously interested in
doing what the modern, International School architects of the 1950s
and 1960s had failed to do—that is, to explore the constraints—not
restraints—of the cities around them. This exploration resulted in my
practicing in a "classical" vocabulary appropriate to Washington,
D.C., although one that was constructed of modern materials and
technologies.

When I came to New York, I found an entirely different city, one
that is not about procession or spaces or order, but about equality
and entrepreneurial might and commerce.

In New York there have been very few opportunities to create whole
new city environments. Even McKim, Mead, and White, who built
throughout the city, did not have the effect on the larger city plan
the way Burnham did, for example, in Washington or Chicago.
Riverside South, however, represents a rare opportunity in New York,
to create a whole new district, a city-scale place at the water. To
create that place, we have designed its built edge as a wall
expressing a bow—close to the ends, low in the middle. This results
in a distinctive and specific urban form, not just another random
grid of buildings crossing the site. There are qualities of sequence
and procession from the tradition of Washington and its European
precedents, but ones that mesh with the traditional grid of New

8

新しいビルは、その背後から傷をいやし、街が川へ発展しようとするのに合せ
て、快適な成長のパターンを確立させて樹皮のように機能することになるでしょ
う。たとえ、既存の箱のようなビルにはばまれてグリッドは縦横に伸びるこ
とはできないものの、それは、街の最後のエッジとして、ある種の「快方」に
向かうものとなるでしょう。

ネット： では、いくらかその壁も改善できるのですか。

チャイルズ： そうです。街は人間の体に似てなくもない。それは調整でき、
再生でき、そして改善できます。そして都市の仕事に携わる私たちは、傷跡が
見えなくなるように何度も正確に縫い直す外科医に似てなくもないのです。

ネット： コロンバス・センターとリヴァーサイド・サウスに共通して私が
すごいと思うのは、あなた方は、過去10年間にみられる建築家たちとは違って、
社会の方向づけ、都市の環境にたいしてより深い提案を行なっていることです。
あなた方は、1980年代のスタイルからは超然としているように思えてなりませ
ん。

チャイルズ： そうであって欲しいです。しかし今日では、全体の構成に関わ
りのない、自分自身のためのファサードのごまかしがみられ、時々、建築の将
来を想うとがっかりします。私は、ファッションよりもむしろ問題の解決に焦
点を合せた真の建築への回帰を望みます。

はるか歴史をさかのぼってみても、インターナショナル・スタイルのたくさん
の建築家は物事にたいして硬直化しています。彼らはより大きな都市的文脈を
無視しています。私はSOM／ワシントンDCでの仕事を通して都市の環境にい
かに応えていくかについて学んできました。ワシントンは連邦の街、連邦の建
築についての力強いアイコンを含む、強烈なアイデンティティのセンスに満ちた
街なのです。そこで私は1950年代と1960年代のモダーンでインターナショナ
ル・スタイルの建築家たちが街における抑制でなく拘束を学び誤まったことに
大変興味を覚えました。この探求は、ワシントンDCに適した「古典的な」デ
ザイン・ヴォキャブラリィとなって表われました。ただし現代の材料と技術に
よるものなのですが………。

私がニューヨークにきたとき、そこは物事の順序、空間、秩序とはかけ離れた、
機会均等、企画遂行力、そしてビジネスに満ちたまったく異なった街であるこ
とを発見しました。

ニューヨークでは、街全体の新しい環境をつくる機会に恵まれることは稀です。
マッキム・ミード・アンド・ホワイトは、街全体を通してつくりあげていった
ものの、彼らですら、たとえばワシントンやシカゴでバーナムが行なった方法
のような、より大きな街づくりに影響を与えることはありませんでした。しか
し、リヴァーサイド・サウスは水際の街のスケールの新しい地区を創造すると
いうきわめて稀な機会となりました。

その空間をつくりだすために、私たちは建物を弓のように、両側は閉じ中央部
は低くなっている壁としてデザインしました。この結果、たんに敷地を横切る
ランダムな格子状の建物ではなく、特色のある都市の姿となって表われていま
す。ワシントンやヨーロッパの前例にみられる伝統からの進化、シークエンス
の質が多々みられ、そしてそれはニューヨークの伝統的なグリッドとかみあっ
ています。街のコンテクストとスケール、それはニューヨークを他のほとんど
の都市と違えています。それはたとえば非対称性や中心から周囲への変化を強

7–*Riverside South.*
8–*Riverside South.*
9–*Columbus Center:*
  computer drawing.
10–*Columbus Center:*
  computer drawing.
11–*View of Worldwide Plaza*
  from the Hudson River.
  Photo by Addison Thompson.
12–*Tribeca Pedestrian Bridge.*
13–*Tribeca Pedestrian Bridge:*
  the elevator tower to the
  side of the bridge.

7-リヴァーサイド・サウス。
8-リヴァーサイド・サウス。
9-コロンバス・センター：コンピュー
  タ・ドローイング。
10-コロンバス・センター：コンピュー
  タ・ドローイング。
11-ハドソン川から見たワールドワイド・
  プラザ
12-トライベカ・ペデストリアン・ブリッジ。
13-トライベカ・ペデストリアン・ブリッ
  ジ：橋詰のエレヴェータ・タワー。

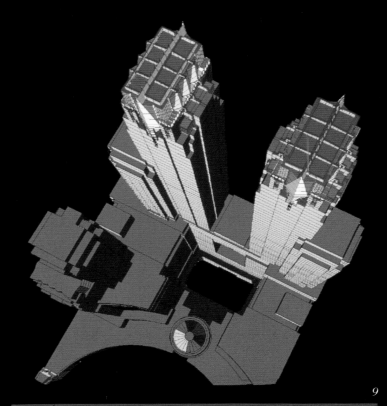

9

10

York.

There's context, a scale, that differentiates New York from almost any other city. It is, for instance, quite different from Tokyo where the emphasis is on asymmetry and diversity from center to periphery.

When a designer solves one problem of scale that does not mean the designer has solved all problems of scale. In New York the issues of scale are very complex; in thinking about a project, there may be one scale appropriate for the whole and other scales appropriate for components of the project. In fact, it may be that the expression of a building's detail heralds its success. For instance, the crown of New York's famous Chrysler Building is one scale, but the expression of the lobby details is quite another.

Sennett: You raise a fundamental issue about urban design. That is the ground-floor level as a design problem, divorced from what happens when you go up, even up one story. In New York, this zone is the intersection of two grids, one vertical and the other horizontal. Yet the design problem is how to rupture between the horizontal and the vertical.

Childs: Even though I had grown up in New York, I saw it with fresh eyes when I moved back here in 1985. I was overwhelmed by the wonders of the city. It made me want to work with the icon of the skyscraper as opposed to the banal reality of the high rise. That was my pursuit when I became the designer for Worldwide Plaza, a rare full-block development in Midtown Manhattan. It includes an office tower, a set of residential buildings, and a large public plaza in between—all located on the "crossbelt" of Manhattan between the East River and the Hudson River, two blocks west of the great urban project, Rockefeller Center.

But I reacquainted myself with New York's old buildings, I realized that they, too, often failed at the ground level. Traditionally, each of these old buildings was in plan a grid within the city grid, so once you entered the building you were in an interior grid. You enter in mid-block and come to a lobby with the elevator banks at the center. In contrast, for Worldwide Plaza, I decided to bring people in on an internal, elliptical, public pathway that extends the building's perimeter.

Rather than the cruciform plan—such as the New York Life building, one of the "models" for Worldwide Plaza—that drains people off the street into the heart of the building, the new design brings people in, but keeps them always in the light and sight of the street. As a second benefit, the building developer then has four distinct building entrances to assign to four separate tenants, giving each a feeling of identity and proprietorship.

Sennett: What I find particularly interesting about Worldwide Plaza is the juxtaposition of the monumentality of the tower and the lower residential component. It changes the block from a row of facades to a space with interior density, in terms of entrance and exit. That is an experiment that has not been conducted often in New York, though I can't say I entirely like the result.

11

間する東京の街ともまったく異なっています。

デザイナーがスケールのもつある問題を解決しても、それはスケールについてのすべての問題を解決したことにはなりません。ニューヨークではスケールの問題はとても複雑です。あるプロジェクトについて考えてみると、全体に適したひとつのスケールはあるでしょうが、かたやその部分に適した別のスケールも存在します。要するに建物のディテールの表現は、その成功を左右します。たとえば、ニューヨークの著名なクライスラー・ビルの王冠（頂部）はあるスケールからくるものであり、かたやロビーのディテールの表現はまったく別のスケールのものです。

エネット：　あなたは都市デザインについての根本的な問題を提起しました。それはいわば1階レヴェルのデザインの問題が、たとえ1フロアでも上るとまったく別の様相を呈してくるというようなことですね。ニューヨークにおいては、この1階レヴェル廻りは垂直、水平の二つのグリッドの交差するところです。かたや、デザインの問題とは、いかに垂直と水平を裂くかということでしょうが………。

チャイルズ：　私はニューヨークで育ったのですが、それでも、私がここに1985年に戻ったときは、ニューヨークを新鮮な目で見ました。私は街の不思議さに圧倒されました。私は平凡な高層ビルの現実とは反対に、スカイスクレイパーのアイコンをデザインしたいと考えるようになりました。私がマンハッタン・ミッドタウンの、ブロック全体を使ったきわめて稀な開発、ワールドワイド・プラザのデザインを担当したときにその追究が始まりました。それはオフィス・タワー、住居施設のビル、そしてその間の大きなパブリック・プラザによって構成され、敷地はロックフェラー・センターという素晴らしい都市的プロジェクトの2ブロック西、イースト川とハドソン川の間のマンハッタンの「横断交通ベルト」に面しています。

私はニューヨークの古いビルを知るようになりましたが、それらもしばしば1階レヴェルで失敗していることに気づきました。古い建物の1階においては、伝統的に平面が街のグリッドの一部となっていて、その結果いったん建物に入るや、建物内部のグリッドに組み入れられてしまう。建物の中に入るや、中央部のエレヴェータ・ロビーに到達してしまう。それとは対照的にワールドワイド・プラザでは、私は、建物の周囲を巡る楕円形の建物内の公共歩廊へと人々を導入するようにしました。

ワールドワイド・プラザのひとつのモデルとなったニューヨーク・ライフ・ビルディングは人々を街路から建物の中心部に吸い寄せる十字形の平面となっていますが、それよりもむしろ今回の新しいデザインは人々に、常に街路の光景と光を意識させながら内部へと導入します。二番目の利点として、この建物のディヴェロッパーは四つのテナントに四つの別個の玄関を与えて独立性と所有権を感じさせることもできます。

セネット：　私がワールドワイド・プラザについてとりわけ興味深く思うのは、タワーと、低層の住居施設をモニュメンタルに並列して配置していることです。それは玄関や出入口という観点からも、建物をファサードの連続体というより、充実した内部の空間へと変化させます。それは結果的にすべてよいとはいえないまでも、ニューヨークではあまり見受けられない実験的試みといえます。

チャイルズ：　ワールドワイド・プロジェクトのデザイン・フェイズの間に挑

Childs: One of the battles during the design phases of the Worldwide project was how the interior space would relate to the public entrances for the entire project and in fact whether the plaza space would serve as the entrance to all the residential units in the overall project. This was one battle where I did not prevail; in the end the proposed entrance for the housing became the pedestrian entrance to the parking, thus diminishing its symbolic use.

Sennett: You seem to have a clear set of ideas about the "urban horizontal" that appears in your work. Is this something that you have thought through consciously?

Childs: Yes, I have, and the development of those principles is inextricably woven with my career at SOM, which I joined as a young architect in 1972 after first working with Nat Owings and Pat Moynihan on the Pennsylvania Avenue Plan. SOM was created over 55 years ago; it represented a new classicism in a way, a style that was later labeled "International School."

In the 1980s, after decades of practice within this single stylistic direction, individual partners within the firm began to explore other expressions. The emerging diversity was confusing because the singular image of SOM was being challenged.

Louis Skidmore and Nathaniel Owings founded the firm in 1936; Merrill, who was an engineer, joined their partnership in 1939. Bunshaft arrived shortly after the founding and was the firm's dominant design force during much of his career. He was located in SOM's New York office, rather than in the original office in Chicago, and it was his design for Lever House that really put the firm on the map. With that project, SOM reformulated the New York office building and produced a wave of development; we changed all of Park Avenue.

Important as SOM's formulation of the office buildings itself proved to be, it nonetheless failed to fully deal with many other issues that personally interested me. For instance, I wanted to design to address the specific aspects of Park Avenue and not just the building plot; I wanted to explore buildings in terms of the evolution of their contexts. These contexts were so rich and vital that I wanted to magnify them.

As SOM's next generation of designers, like me, started to reach out for new expressions and issues, we did not go in one direction; we were going everywhere, in many directions. I found that diversity enormously exciting, and I still do. SOM is a partnership of individuals, each expressing himself within a group structure that enables him to reach beyond the limits of one person. For instance, it allows our architects to take on projects on scales that would simply be impossible for smaller firms. I think there is a power in that diversity that allows greater opportunity to deal with the real issues of architecture than permitted by any singular approach.

Even within my own work I embrace diversity. I think people are sometimes surprised by the many expressions rather than a singular ideology exhibited in my designs. Architecturally, I "grew up" in the world of New Haven, Connecticut, where I particularly admired the

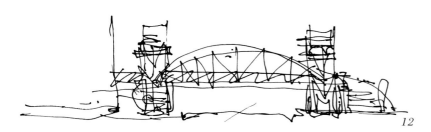

12

戦したことのひとつに、いかにインテリア空間をプロジェクト全体の公共エントランスと関係づけるか、要するに、プラザのスペースを、プロジェクト全体の住居ユニットのエントランスとして機能させられるかということがありました。これは私が克服できなかったことのひとつとなってしまいました。住居用のエントランスの提案は、最後には駐車場への歩行者入口となり、そのシンボリックな扱い方が弱くなりました。

セネット: その作品の中に表われてくる「都市の水平性」という一連の明快な考えが、あなたにはあるように見受けられます。それは意識的に考えていることですか。

チャイルズ: そうです。これらの考え方の展開は、私が1972年に建築家としてSOMに入社し、ナット・オウィングスとパット・モイニハンと一緒にペンシルヴェニア・アヴェニューの仕事を最初にしたときからずっと引き続き練り上げてきました。SOMは55年以上も前に設立され、ある意味での新しいクラシシズム、後にはインターナショナル・スタイルと呼ばれる様式を表現してきました。このたったひとつのスタイリッシュな方向性を何十年と実践した後、1980年代になって、社内のあるパートナーたちは、別の表現方法について研究を始めました。現われてきた変化は、ときとして混乱させかねないものでした。というのは、SOMの唯一のイメージにたいしての挑戦だったのですから。

ルイス・スキッドモアとナサニエル・オウィングスは1936年にこの会社を設立し、技術者だったメリルは1939年にそのパートナーシップに参加しました。バンシャフトは設立の直後に入社し、その活躍中は社の中心的なデザイナーとなりました。彼はシカゴの初期の事務所よりもむしろ、SOMのニューヨーク事務所を本拠地としました。SOMの名を歴史の1ページに残したレヴァー・ハウスは彼のデザインによるものです。このプロジェクトによってSOMはニューヨークのオフィス・ビルを再編成し、発展の波を興しました。私たちはパーク・アヴェニューのすべてを変えてゆきました。

SOMのオフィス・ビルの再編成が重要であることが示されたにもかかわらず、その他の私個人としては興味ある問題の解決には失敗しました。たとえば、私はパーク・アヴェニューにたんに建物を配置するだけではなく、特別の考えをもって語りかけたいと思っていましたし、コンテクストの進化という観点で研究したいと考えていました。これらコンテクストはあまりに豊かで活気のあるものだったため、私はそれらを拡大したいと思っていました。

私のような、SOMの新しいデザイナーの世代は新しい表現や課題に手を伸ばし始めました。私たちは単一の方向でなくどこにでも、様々な方向に向かって進みます。私は今でも変化とは非常にエキサイティングであると考えます。SOMは個人の集まったパートナーシップであり、個人の限界を越えたところまで自らが到達できる組織構造の中で、自分自身を表現できます。たとえば、小さな会社ではとても不可能な大規模なプロジェクトでも、私たち建築家は携わることができます。私は単調な限られたアプローチではなく、建築の真の問題を扱うことのできるすぐれた機会を許容する変化の中に、ある種のパワーがわきてくると考えます。

私自身の仕事においてさえも私は変化を受け入れます。人々は時々私のデザインに示された単一の観念よりもむしろ様々な表現に驚いています。建築的には私はコネティカットのニューヘヴンという世界で「成長」しましたが、そこで

work of Eero Saarinen—an architect who has eluded easy classification by historians. He was different in his approach of looking at the site and finding the appropriate solution for the given program, which resulted in a variety of expressions. His demonstration of particular site and program specific designs exerted an enormous influence on me.

Sennett: Do you ever build at a more intimate scale?

Childs: I do. I am quite excited about a footbridge, a pedestrian bridge that I designed last year. The purpose of this bridge is to get students and neighborhood residents safely across West Street, a 50-foot-wide roadway that divides the community and public transit system from a new public high school and waterfront park. Although it was a relatively small architectural project, it received a great deal of attention because it was highly visible, it was publicly funded, and it had the important job of providing safe passage for students. The design solution is a simple single span, anchored on either side by a pylon which contains elevator and stair access to the bridge. The two bow trusses are offset from one another to reflect the diagonal of West Street within the rectangular city grid. Between the trusses is the enclosure that will protect pedestrians from the weather during their crossing. The bridge in its imagery recalls the great civil works of America's 19th century and serves as the symbolic northern entry to Lower Manhattan and Battery Park City. Because all elements of the bridge structure are revealed, its design required tremendous attention to detail—another hallmark of SOM over its decades of practice. Although this was a small project for me, it ended up requiring as much attention as some of our largest buildings.

Sennett: It seems that even at this smaller scale the principle of creating wholeness around the individual object operates. That is a principle I see throughout your work. It is contextual without making historical quotes.

Childs: I am not interested at all in simple historicism.

Sennett: Except in the Worldwide Plaza building.

Childs: There is always a danger of exploring things too fully, and perhaps that is what I did at Worldwide Plaza. But I am glad I did it and extremely proud of this attempt to pay homage to the traditional New York "skyscraper." By the time I designed Columbus Center, however, I viewed that project more as an abstracted vision of what the city is all about, not a recreation of carefully researched antecedents.

People ask why I don't produce work that is consistently identifiable to hang my hat on. But what I find more stimulating is taking notes that have been played before in the continuum of urban architecture and rearranging them in new ways to produce a different score, or put more directly, to create a building that is both appropriate and new.

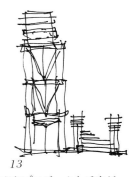

13

は、歴史家による安易な分類をのがれた建築家、エーロ・サーリネンの作品が好きでした。彼は敷地を見、与えられたプログラムへの適切な解決を見つけてゆくそのアプローチにおいて異なっていました。そしてそれは色々な表現方法となって表われました。彼の敷地とプログラムにたいする特殊なデザインの表現は、私に強烈な影響を与えたのです。

セネット： あなたは今までに、より身近な小規模の建築に携わったことがありますか。

チャイルズ： ええ、私は去年デザインした歩道橋にかなりエキサイトしています。その歩道橋の目的は、新しい公立高校やウォーターフロント・パークからコミュニティや新しい交通システムを分断している76mものウェスト・ストリートを、学生や近隣住民が安全に横切れるというものです。

それは建築的には比較的小さなプロジェクトですが、特に周りからよく見え、公共の資本によってつくられ、学生のための安全な通路であるということからかなりの注目を集めました。解決にあたり、両端に設けたエレヴェータと階段の塔にアンカーしたシンプルな単純スパンをデザインしました。二つの弓状のトラスが端から端まで架け渡されてバランスし、街の四角なグリッドの中での斜めのウェスト・ストリートを表現しています。トラスとトラスの間は横断中の歩行者を天候から保護する囲いとなっています。この歩道橋は、イメージとして、19世紀のアメリカの偉大な土木の作品を思い起こさせ、マンハッタンの南、バッテリィ・パーク・シティの北側の入口としてのシンボルとなっています。ブリッジの構造のすべてのエレメントは露出しているため、そのディテールについては細心の注意を払いました。それは過去何十年もの作品を通してもSOMの折り紙つきとなっています。これは私にとって小さなプロジェクトですが、他の大規模プロジェクトと同様の注意を払う必要に迫られました。

セネット： このような小さなスケールにおいても、個人的な目標に関わりながら、全体像を構築する信念が働いているように思えます。それは、あなたの作品を通して見えてくる信念だと思います。

歴史的な引用を伴わないコンテクスト建築なのです。

チャイルズ： 私は単純な歴史主義にはまったく興味がありません。

セネット： ワールドワイド・プラザを除いて、ですね。

チャイルズ： 常に物事を十分に研究しすぎるのは危険ですが、たぶん私はワールドワイド・プラザでそれをやってしまったのでしょう。しかし、私自身そうしたことがうれしいですし、ニューヨークの伝統的な「スカイスクレイパー」に敬意を表するこの試みを誇りに思います。しかし私がコロンバス・センターをデザインするまで、私はこのプロジェクトを、過去のものを十分に研究して再生するのではなく、都市とはこうあるべきものといった、より抽象的な眼指しで見ていました。

人々は、私の証となるような、一貫してアイデンティティある作品をなぜつくらないかと聞きます。しかし私がもっと刺激的であると考えるのは、都市における建築の連続体の中で以前演じられていた流れを引き出し、そして適確で新しい建築をつくりだすために、より直接的で異なった方法によって、それらを再構築することです。

David Childs

Paul Goldberger

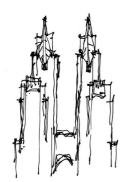

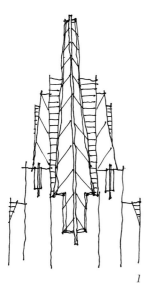

1

There is no such thing as a "David Childs style." It might seem mor
than a little paradoxical that the man who has emerged as the most
powerful presence at Skidmore, Owings & Merrill, a firm known for
the rigor with which it pursued a straightforward, modernist course,
would be an architect so lacking in dogma himself. It is not that
David Childs is anti-modernist, or that he has any lack of respect fo
the heritage of the firm he now commands as SOM's first chairman
(until recently, the partnership was governed by a committee). He is
enthusiastic about what SOM represents, but more because he is
enthusiastic about all architecture of quality than because he shares
the ideological biases that informed his firm from its beginnings
through its mature middle age.

David Childs is an enthusiast, and he has managed with consummate
skill to turn his love for all kinds of architecture into a position of
both power and influence not only within the venerable drafting
rooms of SOM but also in the world outside. Earlier in his career he
was a widely respected member of the Fine Arts Commission in
Washington, D.C.; when he moved to New York, he quickly became
known as an architect who spoke the language of civic groups, of
planners, of urban designers and even, from time to time, of
community groups. A committed centrist, he seemed determined to
forge a synthesis between the esthetic imperatives of architecture
and the pragmatic demands of developers, politicians and citizens.
To a large extent he has succeeded—more so, surely, than any
architect who has practiced in New York in a generation. Indeed, on
almost has to look back to a figure like Daniel Burnham in Chicago
to find an architect who has excercised comparable influence in the
civic realm. Like Burnham, Mr. Childs is widely respected by his
professional colleagues as well as by his corporate clients, and like
Burnham the association of his name with a particular project is
enough to give the project the air of acceptability, if not of total
virtue.

We can surely see that in two major New York City projects, both

2

till unbuilt: Columbus Center, the huge skyscraper planned for the southwest corner of Central Park, and Riverside South, the 76-acre site along the Hudson River that is intended to contain apartments for 12,000 residents and a 21-acre riverside park. Each of these immense projects was initially designed by another architect whose plans elicited violent opposition from critics and civic activists; in both cases the developers turned to Mr. Childs, who produced a scheme that appeared to mollify all sides. (The Columbus Center design was actually a reworking of a Childs scheme for the site that had failed to win acceptance in an initial design-build competition, but had received more respectful reviews than the Moshe Safdie design that won. The Riverside South design was also a kind of reworking; Mr. Childs was brought in to give physical form to a schematic design for the site that had been commissioned by various civic groups in response to earlier schemes they had opposed. The groups eventually convinced the developer to reject the original design in favor of their alternative.)

David Childs has thus become the architect of reconciliation in New York City at this point in its urban-design history. If his position comes in part as a result of temperament—he is easygoing on the surface, determined and self-assured underneath—his ascension to a civic mantle is hardly without some connection to his architecture. As a designer, Mr. Childs's work bespeaks a clear commitment to the values of urbanism: to a preference for seeing buildings not as isolated, abstract objects but as parts of larger wholes, to a commitment to respecting the integrity of the street, and to a willingness to honor the public realm over the private one. Urbanism is his controlling sensibility—it is these values within which the stylistic differences between Mr. Childs's buildings are subsumed. The fact that the handsome Tribeca Bridge, to name one project, is modernist in its stylistic garb, means far less than the fact that it is consciously conceived as a piece of neighborhood fabric, carefully woven to join two disparate portions of downtown.

Columbus Center, Riverside South and Worldwide Plaza—the office and condominium project constructed in the western section of midtown Manhattan—all allude to the classic skyscraper designs of Manhattan between the world wars. Yet these designs seem driven less by nostalgia and sentiment for older architecture than by a belief that the values of urban design should prevail, and that the example of 1920s and 1930s skyscraper design provides a better model for achieving sound urbanism than any modernist model has been able to do.

David Childs believes in the city: this is what unifies his work, and makes it, in the end, as convincing intellectually as any body of work with more stylistic consistency. One sees in all of his projects, not only in New York but elsewhere, the manifestation of a desire that the building be a healing element in the cityscape, not a wounding one; that it connect, not pull apart. In this sense he might be said to have been working in opposition to the unspoken principle that motivated so much of SOM's work in the 1950s and 1960s, the years when the firm made a clear point of elevating the building as object above the city as context. (Sometimes that principle was more than just an attitude, as in the many works of Gordon Bunshaft and other SOM partners that were on platforms, quite literally elevated above the city and set apart from the street.) David Childs's early work in Washington, D.C., represents SOM's first significant retreat from this approach. If many of his Washington buildings, like 1300 New York Avenue, the Grand Hotel, and the Park Hyatt Hotel, were less than refined in their details, they made an essential point: that it was possible for the nation's preeminent corporate architecture firm to design in a manner that acknowledged urban context, that respected the street, and that even allowed itself the indulgence of certain historical borrowings. Mr. Childs's willingness to use historical form has surely made him a fellow traveler of the architects of the post-modern movement, yet he has never seemed fully a part of this amorphous group, either. Unlike

Philip Johnson, for whom historical allusion was primary and urbanism all but ignored, or Michael Graves, for whom collage-like composition came first, Mr. Childs has seemed always to use history as a vehicle toward urban design. Classical columns, cornices and domes were but a means of achieving urbanistic presence, not an end in themselves.

All the more so in New York. Mr. Childs's first major New York project, Worldwide Plaza, is a striking mix of crudeness and elegance, a clear reflection, one suspects, of the economic difficulties of building with serious architectural intentions at large scale in midtown Manhattan. Yet it has an unmistakable presence, not only as a convincing work of urban design but also as a well-meaning piece of architecture. It is difficult to speak of a 1.5-million square foot office tower and 661 apartments as representing a kind of earnest friendliness, but this complex does.

At 450 Lexington Avenue, an office tower, the same air of relaxed ease exists, this time with a somewhat less literally historicizing tone. A playful geometric top in a pattern of diamonds culminates a stepped-back profile, and it comes both in welcome relief to the more ornate skyscraper tops of recent years and as an acknowledgement of the full scope of this building's complicated skyline context, which includes the Chrysler Building, the Pan Am Building, the Helmsley Building and the Chanin Building. Mr. Childs seems to have had something to say to all four, as well as to be making with a certain wit the point that it is possible to design a flat-topped skyscraper and still be inventive.

There is more self-conscious invention to Mr. Childs's only modernist tower in New York, 1540 Broadway, which not entirely convincingly alludes to the deconstructionist mode. (It should be mentioned that several of Mr. Childs's more recent modernist schemes, such as the Gap Headquarters in San Francisco, Logan Airport in Boston, and the Navy Command Center in Washington, D.C., show more elegance and refinement.) If the 1540 Broadway tower has any strength, it is

the way in which its solid base, erector-set-style pinnacle and lavish signage manage to sit comfortably amid the chaos of Times Square—more comfortably, surely, than anything else built so far at Times Square at this huge scale.

Will Columbus Center and Riverside South work as well? It is difficult to tell. Columbus Center owes a major debt to the twin-towered Central Park West apartment buildings of the 1930s, most particularly the Century, but for all the appeal of this building in model and drawing form, it is difficult to believe that it will sit as gently on the cityscape as its predecessor. Riverside South is a masterwork of urban design, a brilliant synthesis of park, highway, street and towers, but here, too, the scale poses a tremendous risk: is very, very big, and there has never been any guarantee in architecture that ideas put through an enlarging machine will emerge unscathed.

If there is any Childs design at very large scale than one truly regrets not seeing realized, it is the scheme Mr. Childs did in association with Frank Gehry for the site of Madison Square Garden and Pennsylvania Station in midtown Manhattan. Here, two architect who might be thought of as precise opposites—Mr. Childs the consummate corporate practitioner, Mr. Gehry the rough-and-tumble *artiste*—joined forces to produce a pair of high-rise office towers joined by grand public space that would have served as the entrance to an improved Pennsylvania Station. Here, David Childs designed an exuberant, lively tower, allowing himself to be goaded by Frank Gehry toward great sculptural potency, even as he proved himself able to move Mr. Gehry toward order. The two architects carved out a point of intersection for their work that could not have been imagined, and which could have been one of the great exclamation points of the skyline.

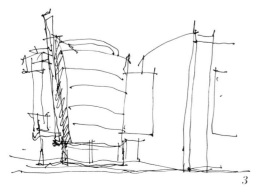

3

1-*Columbus Center*.
2-*Riverside South*.
3-*American Business Center, Berlin*.
4-*Madison Square Garden*.
5-*Istanbul Cultural and Art Center*.

1-コロンバス・センター。
2-リヴァーサイド・サウス。
3-アメリカン・ビジネス・センター、ベルリン。
4-マディソン・スクエア・ガーデン。
5-イスタンブール文化芸術センター。

イヴィッド・チャイルズ
ール・ゴールドバーガー
田明彦訳

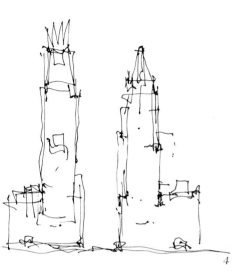

4

デイヴィッド・チャイルズのスタイルのようものは過去にその例をみない。厳格さによって知られ、またそれによって明快で、モダーンな道を歩んできたスキッドモア、オーウィングス・アンド・メリル（SOM）において、最も強力な存在として表われた彼が、実はSOMの教理の面でかつて存在しえなかった建築家であるとはいささか逆説的であるように思われる。デイヴィッド・チャイルズは、反モダニストではなく、また、彼が、今初代会長として指揮しているSOMが培ってきたものにたいする尊敬心が欠如しているわけでもない（最近まで、パートナーシップは役員会によって管理されていた）。彼はSOMが何を主張するかということに熱烈な関心をもっている。それはSOMの初期から成熟期に育てられたイデオロギー的偏見を彼が共有しているからではなく、彼があらゆる質の建築についてきわめて熱心であるからである。

デイヴィッド・チャイルズは、熱狂者である。彼は完璧な手段を駆使してあらゆる種類の建築への情熱を、SOMの設計室ばかりか外部の世界においても、力と影響力のある形へと変えてきた。彼の経歴の初期の段階においてはワシントンDCの芸術委員会において広く尊敬されたメンバーであった。ニューヨークに移るとすぐに彼は、市民、プランナー、都市デザイナー、そしてときに応じて市民グループの言葉を話す建築家として知られるようになる。中道派として、彼は建築の美的欲求と、実務的なディヴェロッパー、政治家、市民の要求の間に立って統合・調整役を決意しているようにみえる。

確かに彼は、他の同世代のニューヨークで活躍するどの建築家よりも、広い領域でより成功してきた。まさに、市民の領域において彼に匹敵した影響力をもつ建築家として、シカゴのダニエル・バーナムのような人物を振り返る必要がある。バーナムのように、チャイルズ氏はプロフェッショナルな同僚と同時にクライアントたちによって、広く尊敬されており、また、バーナムのように、彼の名のついた特別プロジェクトは、そのプロジェクトを許容する雰囲気を醸しだすには十分である、すべてが長所ではないにしても……。

以上のことは、まだ未完ではあるが、次の二つのニューヨーク・シティ大プロジェクトにみることができる。ひとつはセントラル・パークの南西隅に計画されている巨大な超高層、コロンバス・センターであり、またひとつは、ハドソ

ン川に沿った30ha余の敷地に、1万2,000戸の住居をもつアパートと8.5ha余の川沿いの公園を含めたリヴァーサイド・パークである。これら超大型プロジェクトは、それぞれ初期の段階では他の建築家たちによって設計されていたが、それら計画案にたいし、批評家や市民団体が猛烈な反対運動を展開していた。いずれのケースもディヴェロッパーはチャイルズ氏へ依頼した結果、彼はすべての意見を包含するアイデアを提案した（コロンバス・センターのデザインは、実際は、初期の設計競技の段階で落選したチャイルズ案を再検討したものであり、設計競技で当選案となったモシェ・サフディ案よりもさらに高い評価を与えられていた。リヴァーサイド・サウスのデザインもやはり、ある種の再検討案である。市民グループが反対した当初の案にたいして、彼ら自身が選んだ計画案に建築的形態を与えるため、チャイルズ氏はこのプロジェクトに巻き込まれることになる。市民グループは、ディヴェロッパーにたいし、自分たちの代替案のために初期の案を拒否するよう、最終的に納得させることができた）。

デイヴィッド・チャイルズはこのように、ニューヨークのこの時点での都市デザインの歴史において、調停の建築家となった。彼のこの評価は、部分的にせよ彼の性格からくるものであり——彼は表面上はのんきであるが、本質は決然としていて自信家である——、市民のための調停の建築家としてのこのステイタスは、ほとんど彼の建築とは関わりのないところからきている。デザイナーとしてのチャイルズ氏の作品は、建物を単体としての抽象的なオブジェではなく、総体の一部としてみる眼差し、街路の雰囲気を維持し尊重する考え、そして個人の範囲を越えて公共の領域を優先する意志、こうしたアーバニズムの価値にたいする明確なコミットメントを示している。

アーバニズムは彼の統制された感性である。この価値の中に、チャイルズ氏の建物のスタイルの差異がすべて包含される。プロジェクトをたとえてあげれば、ハンサムなトライベカ・ペデストリアン・ブリッジは、そのスタイルにおいて現代的であるというよりも、実は、地域を構成する一要素として意識的に考慮され、二つの異なる地域を注意深く結び付けているという点が注目されるべきである。マンハッタン中西部に建設されたオフィスとコンドミニアムのプロジェクト、コロンバス・センター、リヴァーサイド・サウス、そしてワールドワ

イド・プラザ、これらすべては、二つの世界大戦の間に建てられた古典的なスカイスクレイパーのデザインを暗示している。にもかかわらず、これらは古い建築へのノスタルジーや感性からではなく、都市デザインの価値がまさるべきであるという考え方、また20年代、30年代のスカイスクレイパーのデザインがモダニストが成し遂げようとしたモデル以上に健全な都市を達成するモデルとなるという信念によって、デザインされている。

デイヴィッド・チャイルズは街を信じている。これが、彼の作品を統一する信念であり、一貫したスタイルの作品を、最終的には誰にも知性的に納得させるものとなっている。建築は、街の風景として、心を傷つけるものではなく癒す要素となるべきであり、また、建築は引きはがすものではなく結び付けるものであるという意志を、彼のニューヨークばかりでなく他の地域も含めたあらゆる作品に見出すことができる。こうした意味において、彼は、建築を街の環境におけるオブジェとして位置づけるという明快な点を確立していた50年代、60年代のSOMの作品に貫いていた無言の原理とは、好対照の作品をつくりつづけているということがいえるかもしれない（その無言の原理は、ゴードン・ノンシャフトや他のSOMのパートナーたちによる、プラットフォームに立ったような建築、文字どおり街の上に、街路から浮いて立つ建築に見られるような、単なるジェスチュア以外の何ものでもない）。

デイヴィッド・チャイルズのワシントンDCにおける初期の作品は、SOMのこのアプローチからの、初期の重要な変調の兆しを示している。1300ニューヨーク・アヴェニュー、グランド・ホテル、パーク・ハイアット・ホテルといった彼のワシントンでの様々な建築は、仮にそのディテールにおいて洗練されていないとしても、本質的な点を投げかけている。それは、アメリカの卓越した建築設計事務所が、都市のコンテクストを意識する方法、街路の重要性を尊重する方法、また、ある歴史的な引用の恩恵を許容する方法をとりながらデザインすることが可能であるという点である。チャイルズ氏の歴史的形態をあやつる意志は、たしかに彼をポスト・モダンの潮流における一体験者にしているが、かといって、このついに結晶化されなかったグループの一員には、十分になりきれていないようである。歴史的引喩が第一義的であり、都市はほとんど無視す

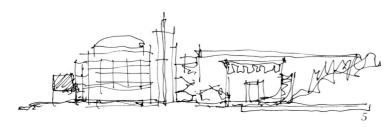

5

ィリップ・ジョンソンと違い、また、コラージュのような構成がまず優先される
マイケル・グレイヴスと違って、チャイルズ氏は、歴史を常に都市デザイン
にたいする機動力としてあつかっているようである。古典的な柱もコーニス
円屋根も、単に都市における存在感を達成するための手段であり、自己完結
に終るものではない。

ューヨークにおいては、より以上、その傾向にある。チャイルズ氏の最初の
ューヨークの大プロジェクト、ワールドワイド・プラザは、未完成と洗練さ
顕著に混じりあい、ミッド・マンハッタンの巨大プロジェクトにおいて正面
った建築提案を行う際に直面する、様々な経済的な問題を如実に反映してい
。にもかかわらず、それは説得力のある都市デザインとしてばかりでなく、
味深い建築作品として、まちがいのない存在感を与えている。14万㎡のオフ
ス・タワー、および661戸のアパートが、温かく、親みやすいものとして語ら
るのは往々にしてむずかしいが、このプロジェクトは違う。

0レキシントン・アヴェニューのオフィス・タワーも、文字どおりの古典的な
いはやや影をひそめてはいるものの、同様のゆったりした雰囲気を醸しだし
いる。ダイヤモンド状のパターンを示す、陽気な幾何学的な頂部は、しだいに
頂上にゆくにしたがってセットバックし、それはここ数年のより華美なスカ
スクレイパーを歓迎するレリーフであると同時に、また、クライスラー・ビル、
ン・アメリカン・ビル、ヘルムズリー・ビル、チェイニン・ビルといった、この
築を取りまく複雑なスカイラインをもつコンテクストを許容するものとなっ
いる。チャイルズは、これら四つのタワーに何かいいたげな様子であり、ま
、平たい屋根のスカイスクレイパーのデザインは可能ではあるが、さらに工
すべきであるということを、ウィットに富んで指摘しているように見える。
チャイルズ氏の唯一のモダニストとしてのタワー、ニューヨークのワン・ブロ
ードウェイ・プレイスには、より自分を意識した工夫があるが、それは、デコ
ストラクションの流儀を十分に語ってはいない（サンフランシスコのGAP本
ビル、ボストンのローガン空港、ワシントンDCのアメリカ海軍コマンド・セ
ターといった、チャイルズ氏の最近のいくつかのモダニストとしてのスキー
は、より上品で洗練されているということができる）。ワン・ブロードウェイ・

プレイス・タワーの力強さは、そのソリッドな基壇、直立した小尖塔、そして
あの誇張されたサインがタイムズ・スクエアの混屯の中に何とか心地よく居座
っているからであり、であるからこそ、今までにタイムズ・スクエアに建てら
れたこの種のいかなる巨大プロジェクトよりも、より気持ちよく、確かな存在
となっている。

コロンバス・センターも、リヴァーサイド・サウスも同様な効果が期待できる
か？　それはむずかしい判断である。コロンバス・センターは、今世紀を代表
する1930年代のトゥイン・タワーであるセントラル・パーク・ウェスト・アパ
ートにたいし、大変な負い目を負うている。模型や図面でその形態を十分見て
も、その前任者と同様に、街の風景として優しく居座っているとはいいがたい。
リヴァーサイド・サウスは、公園、高速道路、街路、そしてタワーがうまく統
合したアーバン・デザインの名作であるが、ここにもそのスケールが非常なリ
スクを負っている。それはあまりにも巨大すぎて、肥大化するマシーンを通り
抜けた建築のアイデアが無傷のまま現出できるといういかなる保証もないこと
を物語っている。

チャイルズの大規模プロジェクトのデザインの中で、その実現を見ずに惜しま
れるのは、ミッド・マンハッタンのマディソン・スクエア・ガーデンとペンシ
ルヴェニア駅の敷地に、フランク・ゲーリィと協力して行なったスキームであ
る。ここでは、完璧な組織の運営者であるチャイルズ、荒唐無稽な「芸術家」
であるゲーリィ、このまったく対照的であると考えられているような建築家ど
うしが、超高層のトゥイン・タワー・オフィスとともに、改修されるペンシル
ヴェニア駅のエントランスとして使われる大きなパブリック・スペースをつく
ろうと力を合せた。ここでデイヴィッド・チャイルズは、フランク・ゲーリィ
の彫刻的なデザインに煽動されることを自ら許しながら、華麗でにぎやかなタ
ワーをデザインしたが、と同時にゲーリィにたいしても、建築のオーダーに従
わせることができるという証明をも行なった。二人の建築家は、実現すること
はなかったが、驚嘆すべきスカイラインとして永く記憶に残る作品をとおして、
両者の接点としての形態を刻みこんでいる。

Selected New York Projects

Six Projects for New York City

Marilyn Jordan Taylor

ニューヨーク・シティ 6 プロジェクト

マリリン・ジョーダン・テイラー

高木義雄訳

1　*2*

From Central Park to the Empire State Building, from the Statue of Liberty to the Hell Gate Bridge, New York City has long served as site for many of the world's most remarkable civic and architectural works. In this exuberant and entrepreneurial world city, architecture is stage-set as well as object, image as well as function, and metaphor as well as reality. The six projects by David Childs, featured in this section, portray the challenge and rewards of designing in and for New York.

Riverside South (1) clings to the Hudson River, New York City's fjord. Here salt marshes once cleansed the city's surface water, only to be transformed by the arrival of the region's vast industrial railroad system. As that use was superseded by highways and air freight, the land deteriorated to an inaccessible and unusable state. This new project, which will introduce 5700 residential units, a center for television and movie filming, streetfront shopping, and an expansive riverfront park, extends the city grid in neighborhood-scale blocks and restores the river edge to its true owners, the city's residents. Riverside South exemplifies a crucial urban priority: reclaiming former industrial lands as living neighborhoods and active open spaces.

At Columbus Circle (2), the southwest corner of the sweeping space of Central Park, four diverse neighborhoods meet. Commercial Midtown, low- and moderate-income Clinton, residential and cultural Upper West Side, and the city's most-renowned and best-visited park join in one special geometric form which interrupts the grid and allows Broadway to slice northward. The architectural challenge of Columbus Center is the vertical integration of a multiplicity of urban uses—parking, retail, movie theaters, offices, and residences totaling over 2.5 million square feet—while achieving spaces completely workable for each. The urban design challenge is making the development not only an acceptable reuse of the site but also a key linchpin that will bring its disparate adjoining neighborhoods together.

Park Avenue remains New York's premier address, but several of its buildings have reached the end of their economic life. Many are architectural landmarks that will be renewed. Others, like 320 Park Avenue (3), are 1960 office buildings of undistinguished character, whose enclosure, mechanical and electrical systems are outmoded and unable to achieve the required performance standards of the 21st century workplace. This development project will reshape both the function and image of the building, retaining 660,000 square feet of leasable space but resizing floorplates and replacing all major

セントラル・パークからエンパイア・ステイト・ビルディングへ、自由の女神からヘルゲイト・ブリッジへ。ニューヨーク・シティは、世界の主要な都市的かつ建築的作品を継続的に生みだしてきた。この生気溢れた企業家の世界都市において、建築は実体であると同時に舞台のセットであり、機能であると同時に偶像であり、実在であると同時に隠喩でもある。この章で紹介するデイヴィッド・チャイルズによる六つのプロジェクトは、ニューヨークにおいて、そしてニューヨークのために彼が挑戦し、勝ちえたデザインの記録である。

リヴァーサイド・サウス（1）はハドソン川、ニューヨークのフィヨルドのほとりにある。ここはかつて塩沼で工業用の鉄道用地として干拓された場所であった。後にその用途は高速道路や航空用地へと変化したが、その敷地はますます近づきがたく無用なものになりさがっていた。この新しいプロジェクトには、5,700の住戸とテレビ局や映画館、通り沿いの店舗や広々とした臨海公園が計画された。敷地には近隣と同じスケールの街区のグリッドを拡張し、その真に所有者たる都市の住民に川端の生活を取り戻させた。リヴァーサイド・サウスは、都市生活における決定的な優先順位を例証している。古い工業用地を近隣の住民のために再生させ、活気のある公共空間にすべきだ、ということを。

コロンバス・サークル（2）はセントラル・パークを展望する南西の一角にあり、それぞれに性格の異なる四つの地域が接する場所である。商業地域のミッドタウン、低中所得層の集まるクリントン、文化的住宅地域のアッパー・ウェスト・サイド、そしてこの街の最も有名で訪れる人の多い公園の四つにより構成される幾何学的なグリッドをブロードウェイがつき破り、北方へすりぬけてゆく地点である。コロンバス・センターにおける建築的な挑戦は多様な都市の用途――駐車場、店舗、映画館、オフィス、住宅それら総計23万㎡を越える施設――を垂直方向に統合し、かつ各々の空間を完全に機能させることであった。また、この都市デザインにおける挑戦は敷地の無難な再利用に終わることなく、それぞれに異なる隣接地域を融合させる鍵となるくさびをつくることであった。

パーク・アヴェニューはニューヨークの創世紀の地域であるが、その中のいくつかの建物は経済的な価値の終焉に達してしまっている。それらの多くは建て替えられる運命であることを自ら示すランドマークでもある。しかし、それ以外の、たとえば320パーク・アヴェニュー（3）のようなものは、1960年代に建てられたありふれたオフィス・ビルであり、機械や電気のシステムが時代遅れで、21世紀の執務スペースとして要求される基準点には達しえないものである。しかし、この開発プロジェクトにおいてこの建物は機能とイメージ両面において再生される。約6万㎡の賃貸店舗スペースに上床を施し、主要な機械をすべて入れ替えるだけではなく、パーク・アヴェニューの新しいランドマークとしての外観も創造する。かくして時代から取り残されたものが、追いやられたり

3

4　　　5

6

1-Riverside South.
2-Columbus Center.
3-320 Park Avenue.
4-One Broadway Place.
5-Madison Square Garden.
6-Tribeca Pedestrian Bridge.

1-リヴァーサイド・サウス。
2-コロンバス・センター。
3-320 パーク・アヴェニュー。
4-ワン・ブロードウェイ・プレイス。
5-マディソン・スクエア・ガーデン。
6-トライベカ・ペデストリアン・ブリッジ。

uilding systems while also creating a new landmark for Park venue. Thus the outmoded is revitalized rather than left behind or iscarded. A faceless building on a grand urban promenade becomes n identifiable structure that contributes to, rather than relies on, its ddress.

While Park Avenue is reserved, business-like and even sedate, Times quare teems with city life. Changes to city zoning, designed to eflect transportation capacities and to shift Midtown development to he west, called for a massive introduction of new office space in the imes Square District, but in a way that the vibrant retail and ntertainment uses would not be imperiled. The One Broadway Place 4), situated at the northern end of the "bow-tie" of streets that orms Times Square, achieves the double identity that the city oning sought. At its base, it is a multi-story complex of shops and novie theaters, extending the life of the street indoors. Above this ase but entered around the corner is 760,000 square feet of office pace, enjoying sweeping views over the city.

New York Pennsylvania Station—the very name evokes waves of entiment for the loss of one of the city's most revered architectural andmarks, a classic monument that fell victim to redevelopment in he 1960s. But while the building was demolished, the station function was retained and now brings more than 250,000 people to and from New York each day. The proposed project (5), a collaboration of talent and spirit with Frank Gehry, adds two new office towers to the site, while regaining architectural and civic significance for its critical transportation function. Two unique skyscrapers, deep in dialogue with each other and with the city around them, are proposed to tower above, protect, and identify this important city gateway. Regrettably, for the moment at least, this project has proved too grand in scale, even for New York.

At the smaller yet very significant scale, the Tribeca Bridge (6) spans West Street as it enters Lower Manhattan, linking students from across the city with the front door of Stuyvesant High School and linking the residents of adjoining neighborhoods with a new waterfront park. The Tribeca Bridge, an arched truss weighing 285 tons and spanning 250 feet, serves both function and image. In the tradition of the great civic works of the city, it serves not only for passage but also as gateway to a major district of the city that is undergoing change. Its clear message is that the small elements of the civic realm, as well as the large, must be designed in full awareness of their contribution to urban image and place.

て去られたりすることなく再生される。都市の遊歩道にたいして顔をもたな った建物が、その居所により識別されるのではなく、むしろその居所の認識 たいして貢献することができるようになる。

パーク・アヴェニューが控え目で、ビジネスライクで地味でさえあるのにたい 、タイムズ・スクエアは都市的生活に満ち溢れている。市の区画の変更は、 通量を反映し、ミッドタウンの開発を西へ移すべく計画され、タイムズ・ス エア地域における新しいオフィス・スペースの大規模な導入が要請されたが、 気溢れる商業や娯楽施設の利用が危うくならないように考慮された。ワン・ ブロードウェイ・プレイス・ビルディング（4）はタイムズ・スクエアを形成 る「バウ・タイ（蝶ネクタイ）」の北の端に位置し、市の地域制に求められる つのアイデンティティを達成している。建物の基壇は、街路空間を室内に引 入れた何層にも渡る店舗や映画館のコンプレックスである。そしてその基壇 上に 約7万㎡ のオフィス空間がそびえ、そこからは都市を見回し、景色を楽 むことができる。

ニューヨーク・ペンシルヴェニア駅といえば、その名前は、1960年代の再開発 犠牲になったクラシックなモニュメントであり、最も尊敬を集めた建築的ラ ンドマークのひとつを失ったというセンチメンタルな感情の高まりを呼び起こ せる。しかし、建物は破壊されたが駅の機能は存続し、今もなお、毎日2万 5,000人以上の人々をニューヨークの内外に運んでいる。提案されたプロジェク ト（5）は、フランク・ゲーリィの才能と精神との合作であり、二つの新しい オフィス・タワーを敷地に加えることにより、重要な輸送機能に加えて建築的 そして都市的な重要性をも回復させている。二つのユニークな摩天楼は互いに そして取り巻く都市と深く対話しており、塔を高くし安全装置を施し、都市の 重要な玄関である駅を防御し、識別させるべく提案されている。残念ながら、 少なくとも現在のところ、このプロジェクトは、ニューヨークでさえも規模が 大きすぎることがわかっている。

比較的小さいが重要なスケールであるトライベカ・ブリッジ（6）はウェスト・ ストリートへと架かり、ロウア・マンハッタンへ入るものである。この橋は、 スタイヴサント高校の正面玄関と生徒を結ぶものであり、また、新しいウォー ターフロントの公園と近くに住む居住者とを結んでいる。トライベカ・ブリッ ジは285トンの重さ、76m幅のトラスのアーチで、機能とイメージの両方を供し ている。偉大なる都市の作品の伝統の中で、この橋は単なる通過導線ではなく、 今なお変化を続けるこの都市の主要な地域への玄関の役目を果たしている。そ れは、都市の中の小さな要素であっても、大きな領域と同じくらいに都市のイ メージや場所性にたいして寄与していることを、十分認識してデザインはなさ れなければならないということを明瞭に示している。

Six New York Projects: Site Location Map

ニューヨーク 6 プロジェクト位置図

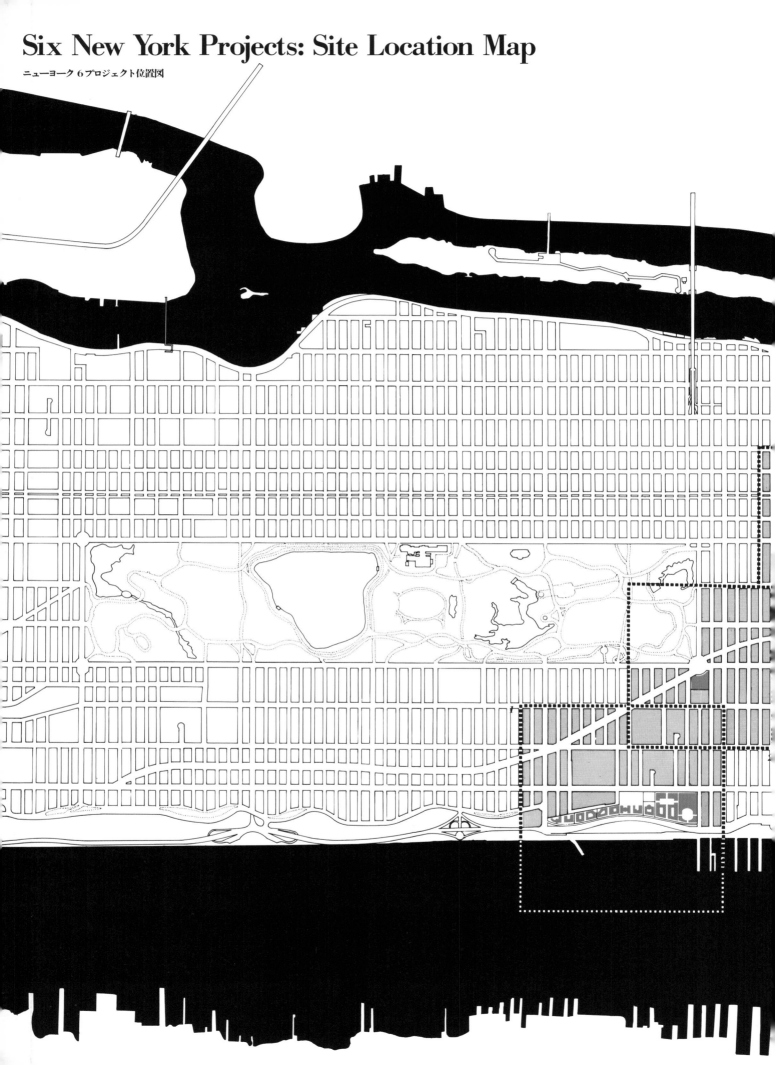

Riverside South

New York, New York
in collaboration with Paul Willen
リヴァーサイド・サウス
ニューヨーク州ニューヨーク
（ポール・ウィリンとの共同設計）
1992

Riverside South is a new urban neighborhood on 55 acres of undeveloped land extending nearly two thirds of a mile along New York City's dramatic western edge, the Hudson River. The site, formerly the location of an extensive, but now abandoned rail freight yard, contains an active rail line for passenger service, an elevated highway, and inaccessible, dilapidated piers. The plan for Riverside South brings the city back to the river by extending the city grid westward and introducing a public park that invites people to the waterfront.

The development program for the site consists of 5,700 dwelling units, neighborhood retail, cultural and community facilities, film studios, and a 21-acre park designed to serve all the residents of the city. To accomplish direct and unobstructed access to the waterfront, the elevated highway is relocated to an inland, at-grade alignment beneath the local streets and the park. The buildings are planned to extend the predominant urban form of the neighborhood, mixing townhouses, streetwall apartment buildings, and slender towers.

リヴァーサイド・サウスは、ニューヨークの西端、ハドソン川に沿って約1km にわたって広がる22ha余の未開発地域にたいする都市の新しい近隣地区計画である。この敷地は以前は広大な鉄道用地であり、現在も使われている旅客用の鉄道や高速道路の高架、また荒廃した埠頭が存する。この計画は水際線を都市へ帰するものであり、そのためにマンハッタンの街区を西側に延長し、都市の住民をウォーターフロントへ呼び戻す遊歩道、および公園を導入するものである。

この計画は5,700戸の住居地区、近隣商業地区、コミュニティ施設、映画撮影所、そしてニューヨーク市民のための8.5haの公園からなる。ウォーターフロントにたやすく近づけるように、高架の高速道路は、街路や公園の下を通り、内陸よりに路線変更される。

建物は、住宅、タウンハウス、街路沿いに建つアパートメント、そしてほっそりしたタワーなどの際立った都市の形態をなして連なるべく構成される。

建物の配置は周囲の環境と応答しながら計画される。敷地を境界づける湾曲する街路は15〜18層の建物の基壇により形づくられる。またその上に立ち並ぶタワーはこの計画全体の形態を決定するものであり、南北の端部が最も高く、公園の幅が最も広い中央部が低くなるよう計画されている。　　　　（高木義雄訳）

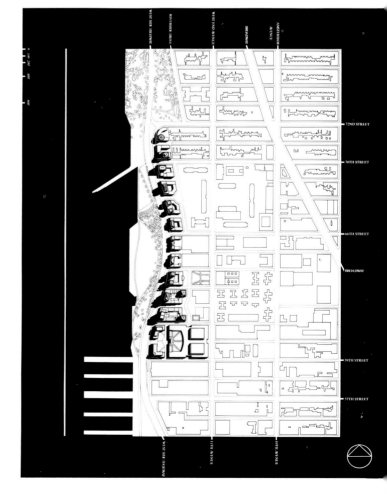

(right)Site plan.　　　　　　　（右）配置図。
(opposite)View from the north.　　（次頁）北側から見る。
Rendering by Richard Rochon.

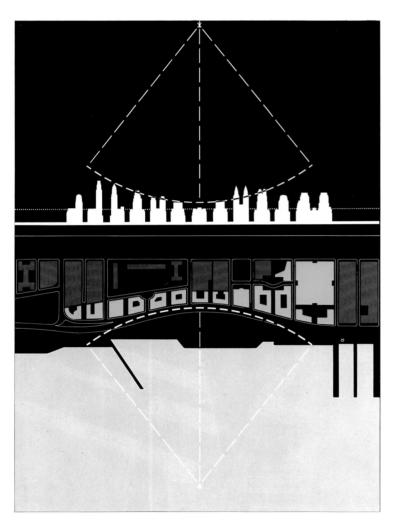

(above left) Conceptual diagram : building massing responds to width of park and curve of Riverside Drive : buidings are lowest where park in widest.

・(左上)概念図：建物のマッシングは公園の奥行きとリヴァーサイド・ドライヴの曲がりぐあいに呼応する。公園の奥行きが最も深いところでは、建物の高さが最も低くなる。

(above right) Axonometric diagram : building massing responds to park and curvilinear drive.

（右上）アクソノメトリック・ダイアグラム：建物のマッシングは公園と湾曲して走る自動車道に呼応する。

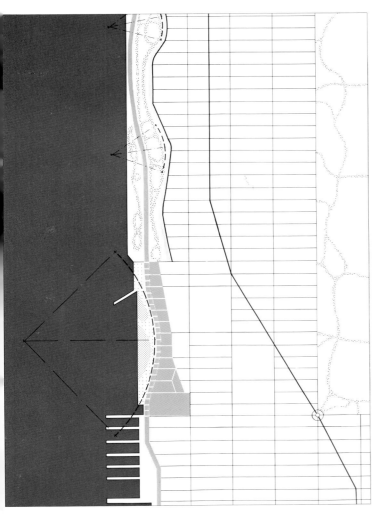

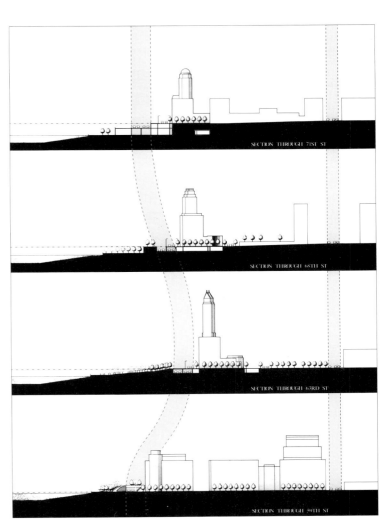

(above left) Space/plan diagram : plan extends curvilinear street wall of existing Riverside Drive.

（左上）空間と平面のダイアグラム：現在直線状のリヴァーサイド・ドライヴを湾曲させ、それに沿って計画が展開する。

(above right) Cross sections illustrate benefits of highway realignment.

（右上）断面図：高速自動車道の路線変更により公園と建築群とのつながりが密になる。

*(above) Elevation : the range
of buildings with various forms
and heights.
(below) Three diagrams : city
street grid extended and
highway realigned.*

（上）立面図：様々の形態と高さをもつ建
築群の連なり。
（下）ダイアグラム：街路のグリッドの拡
張と高速自動車道の路線変更を示す。

Existing condition/現状.

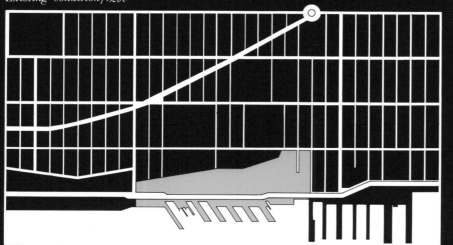

Extension of the Manhattan grid/

マンハッタンの街路グリッドの拡張

Curving of Riverside Drive/リヴァーサイド・ドライヴの湾曲

(above) Existing condition.
(below and opposite top)
Model photos : elevation views
looking east.
Photos by Bryan Nolan.

（上）現状。
（下、次頁上）計画案模型：西から見る。

Columbus Center

New York, New York

コロンバス・センター
ニューヨーク州ニューヨーク

1990

Columbus Center, a two-million-square foot, multi-use complex containing retail, office, residential, and parking facilities will be built on the western circumference of Columbus Circle at the southwest corner of Central Park. The project massing expresses the qualities of the four distinct city neighborhoods: Midtown Manhattan, the Clinton neighborhood, the Upper West Side, and Central Park that converge at this location.

The base, reflecting the sweeping arc of Columbus Circle, is a four-story retail element that continues the pedestrian scale of the streetwall of Broadway and surrounding structures. The intermediate office level, rising to the 21st floor, provides a massing configuration comparable with its context. Three paired, residential towers, rise above the offices, to varying heights, culminating 62 floors above the circle in the central twin towers, reminiscent of the famous twin tower apartments.

Materials and coloration further define the character of this building while responding to its setting. Dark granite at the first floor emphasizes the pedestrian scale of the base-level retail activities. Precast piers become progressively lighter in color as they rise to successive pier caps, softly illuminated at night to enhance the perception of the building as a series of towers. The twin central towers are each capped with a glass formed sentinel, serving as a symbolic compass marker at the skyline, noting this landmark's place as the point of transition for the meshing of the urban fabric of these various Manhattan neighborhoods.

敷地は、セントラル・パーク南西部の角のコロンバス・サークルの西側の縁にあり、面積は18万6,000㎡、商業空間、オフィス、住居、駐車場をもつ多目的な複合施設である。このプロジェクトはミッドタウン・マンハッタン、クリントン近郊、アッパー・ウェストサイドと、セントラル・パークといった四つの近隣地区のそれぞれの特徴を表わすに足る巨大なものである。

基壇部分は、コロンバス・サークルの滑らかな円弧に沿っており、歩行者のスケール感に合わせたブロードウェイ沿いの建物あるいはその周囲の建物に連続する4層の商業空間から成っている。中間部のオフィスは、21階まであり、その外観は、周囲の状況とは際立った、量塊に富む構成となっている。オフィス階の上には、三組の住居タワーがそれぞれ異なった高さで伸び、その中の2棟は、あの有名なトゥイン・タワーのアパートメントを連想させるように62階の高さまで伸びている。

建物は、背景に対応した材料・色使いによってさらに個性的なものになっている。基壇部の商業空間は、1階部分に黒みがかった花崗岩を用いることで、歩行者のスケール感覚に合ったものになっている。プレキャスト製のピアは、柱頭にゆくにしたがって次第に明るくなり、夜にはほのかに輝いて、タワーの輪郭を表わす。中央の二つのタワーの頂部には、それぞれガラス製の標識が取り付き、マンハッタンの建築群が織りなす景色にあって、ランドマーク的な場所であることを示す象徴的な羅針盤の役割を果たしている。　　　　　（河野裕訳）

(right) Site plan.
(opposite) Bird's eye view looking east.
Rendering by Richard Rochon.

(右)配置図。
(次頁)コロンバス・サークルに面した東側を見る。

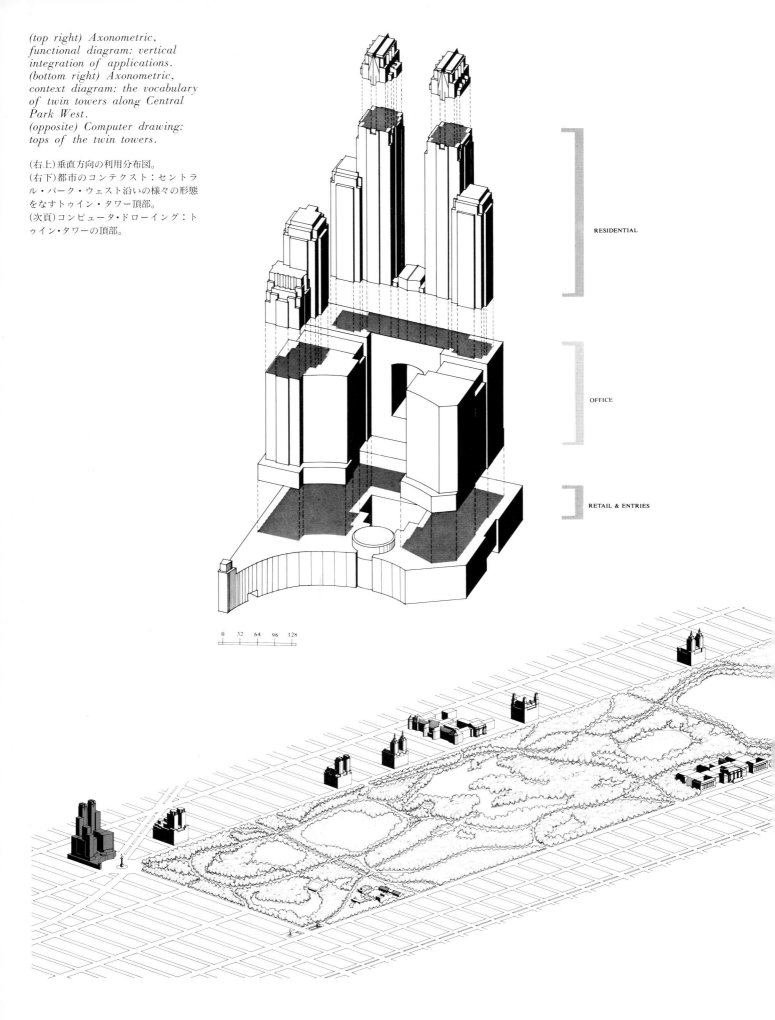

(top right) Axonometric, functional diagram: vertical integration of applications.
(bottom right) Axonometric, context diagram: the vocabulary of twin towers along Central Park West.
(opposite) Computer drawing: tops of the twin towers.

(右上)垂直方向の利用分布図。
(右下)都市のコンテクスト：セントラル・パーク・ウェスト沿いの様々の形態をなすトゥイン・タワー頂部。
(次頁)コンピュータ・ドローイング：トゥイン・タワーの頂部。

RESIDENTIAL

OFFICE

RETAIL & ENTRIES

0　32　64　96　128

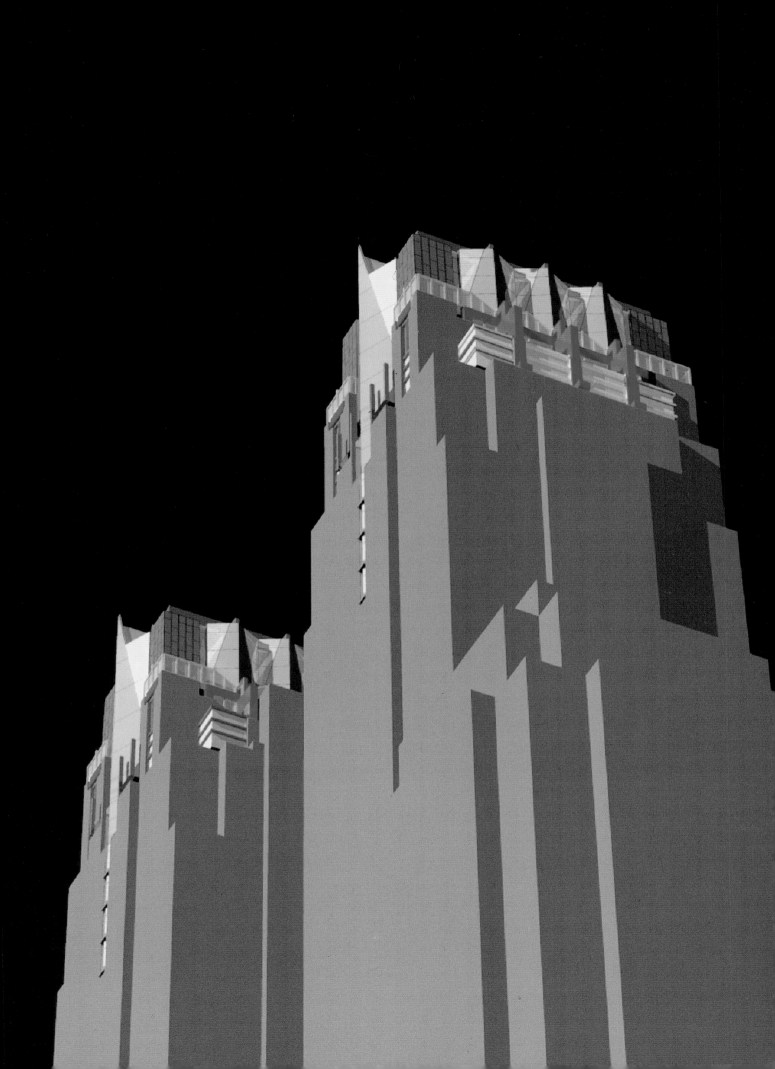

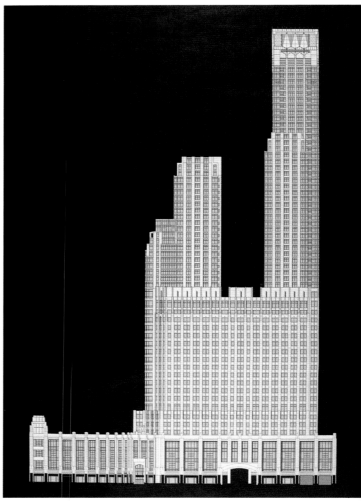

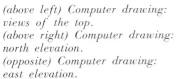

(above left) Computer drawing:
views of the top.
(above right) Computer drawing:
north elevation.
(opposite) Computer drawing:
east elevation.

（左上）コンピュータ・ドローイング：
トゥイン・タワー頂部を見る。
（右上）コンピュータ・ドローイング：
北側立面図。
（次頁）コンピュータ・ドローイング：
東側立面図。

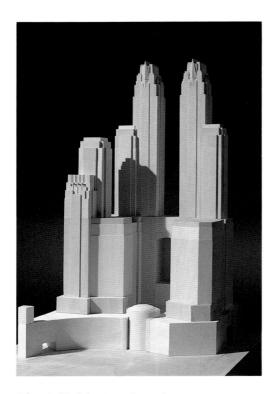

(above) Model: view from the
east.
Photo by Betsy Feeley／SOM.
(right) East-west section.

（上）模型：東側から見る。
（右）東西断面図。

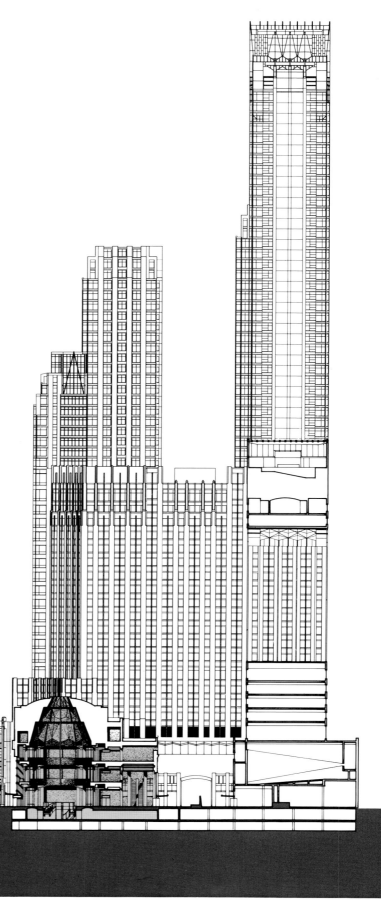

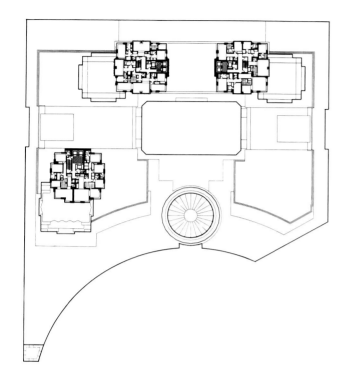

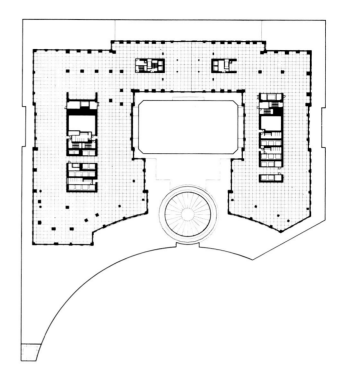

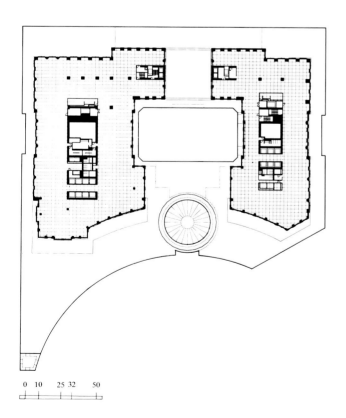

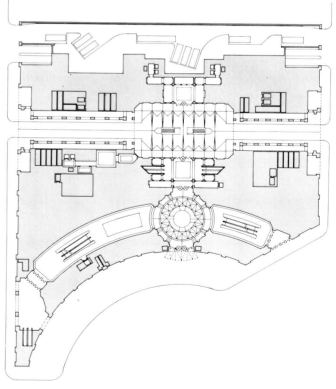

0 10   25 32   50

(top left) Residential levels.
(above left) Midrise office levels.
(top right) Lowrise office levels.
(above right) Ground level.

（左上）住居階平面図。
（左下）オフィス中層階平面図。
（右上）オフィス低層階平面図。
（右下）1階平面図。

(opposite) Office lobby.
Rendering by Richard Rochon.
(below) Axonometric, lobby
sequence.
(right) Courtyard: residence and
office lobby on the ground
floor.
Photo by Betsy Feeley／SOM.

（前頁）オフィス・ロビー。
（下）アクソノメトリック図：ロビーのつ
ながり。
（右）1階コートヤード。オフィス階および
住居階のロビーとなる。

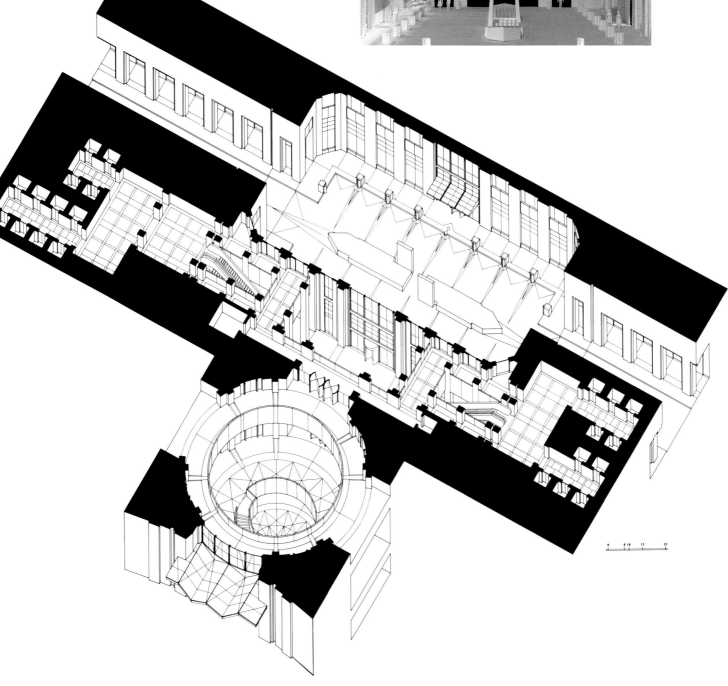

320 Park Avenue

New York, New York

320 パーク・アヴェニュー
ニューヨーク州ニューヨーク
1991

Transforming outdated, non-performing structures into modern, profitable buildings is a current challenge facing many property owners and their architects. The office building at 320 Park Avenue is typical of the "wedding cake" style dictated by the New York City zoning and envelope requirements of the 1950's, providing floorplates substandard for today's technology driven environment. The renovation plans for 320 Park provide more efficient and marketable floorplates by redistributing existing floor area from the base to the mid-rise and high-rise levels. The renovation also replaces the existing curtain walls, updates all structural, mechanical, electrical, and plumbing systems, and accommodates an existing commuter rail right-of-way beneath the building.

The new architectural expression of the building emanates from the renovated lobby and a glass-enclosed entrance pavilion. A lobby richly adorned with marble, onyx, and quality metals is flooded with natural light from a three-story pavilion, the focal point of the building's base. Flanking the entrance pavilion, the black granite clad base provides a platform of solidity and permanence from which the building soars skyward, terminating in a series of pier caps at successive setbacks. The verticality of the towers is further enhanced by integrating granite pilasters with deep, silver-painted mullions. Crowning the building is a three-dimensional translucent glass and metal "tiara", lit by the reflection of sunlight during the day and by internal illumination at night, serving as a beacon within the city's skyline and providing a new point of orientation for Manhattan.

時代遅れの無益なビルを新しく建て替える事業が多くの資産家と建築家の当座の問題である。320 パーク・アヴェニューのオフィス・ビルは、1950年代当時にニューヨークの街に求められたゾーニング・コードに沿った典型的な「ウェディング・ケーキ」の形態をなし、フロア・プランは、今日の技術状況からすると標準以下のものである。320 パーク・アヴェニューの改修計画は、基壇部から中間層あるいは高層部にかけて、現在の床面積を振り分けることで、効率的で市場価値のあるフロア・プランを提案しようというものである。この改修で、現在使われているカーテンウォールも取り替え、構造・機械・電気・配管のシステムを新しくし、建物の直下を通る通勤電車用のパイプラインを調節する。改修後のロビーやガラスで囲まれたエントランス・パヴィリオンから新しい建築的な表情が生まれる。大理石、縞メノウ、良質の金属で贅沢に装飾されたロビーは、建物基壇部の中心となる3層の高さをもつパヴィリオンからの自然光で溢れている。このエントランス・パヴィリオンと側面を接する基壇部は、黒花崗岩が貼られた堅固で耐久性のある台座を形成していて、そこから建物は空に向かってそびえ、徐々にセットバックした壁面のピア頂部で最高点に達する。奥行きが深くて銀色に塗られたマリオンをもつ花崗岩の壁柱が集まって見えることによって、タワーの垂直性が強調される。建物の頂部には、半透明のガラスと金属でできた立体的な「頭飾り」が冠せられていて、日中は太陽の光によって、また夜間は内部の照明によって輝き、街のスカイラインの中で信号灯の役割を果たして、マンハッタンの新たな指標となる。 (河野裕訳)

(right) Site plan.
(opposite) Park Avenue looking south.
320 Park Avenue Tower is visible on the right.
Rendering by Richard Rochon.

(右)配置図。
(次頁)パーク・アヴェニューを南に向かって見る。右手に320パーク・アヴェニュー・タワーが見える。

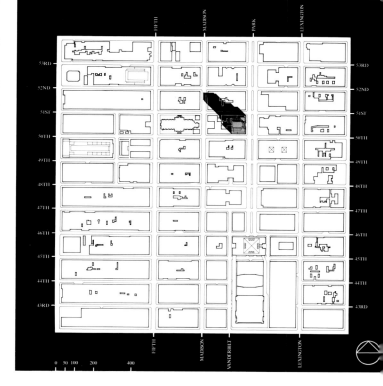

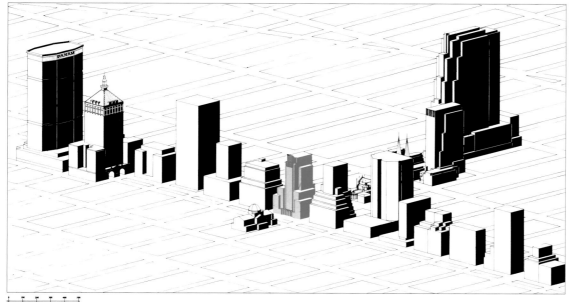

(top left) Conceptual transformation of the building: transformation of 1960s office box into dramatic vertical tower.
(above left) Axonometric, context diagram: reconfigured tower addresses Park Avenue and Rockfeller Center to the west.

(right) Wood models: existing and proposed.
Photos by Betsy Feeley/SOM.
(opposite) View of the front and north facades.
Photos (pp.55,56 and p.58) by Bryan Nolan.

(左上)ダイアグラム：1960年代の建物を動的なタワーに変容させる。
(左下)アクソノメトリック，コンテクスト・ダイアグラム：変容したタワーがパーク・アヴェニューと西側のロックフェラー・センターと呼応する。
(右)木製模型：現状と計画案。
(次頁)正面と北側のファサードを見る。

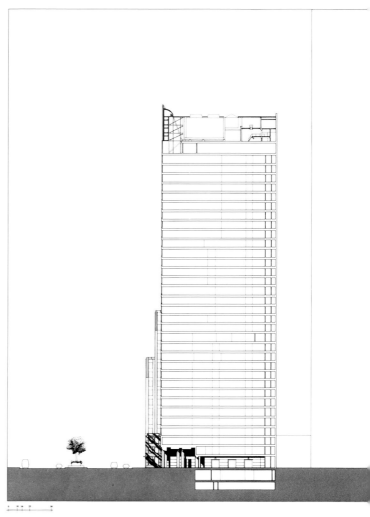

(above left) Night view.
(above right) Section.
(opposite) Axonometric drawing:
top of the building looking up.

（左上）夜景。
（右上）断面図。
（次頁）アクソノメトリック図：タワー頂
部を見上げる。

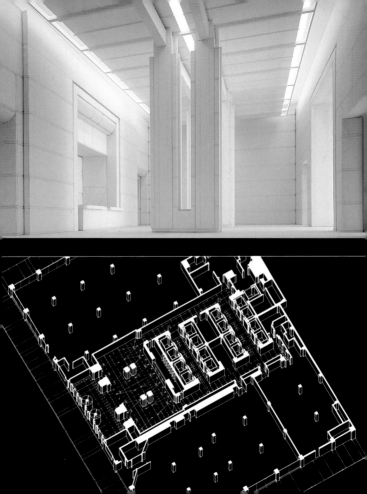

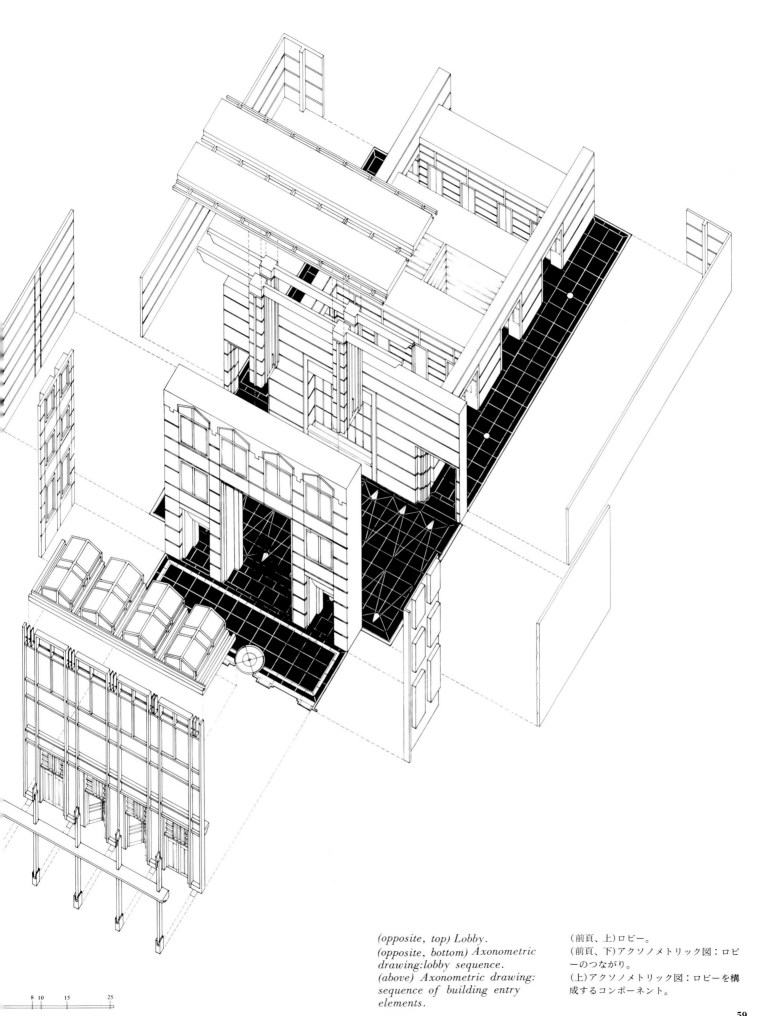

(opposite, top) Lobby.
(opposite, bottom) Axonometric
drawing:lobby sequence.
(above) Axonometric drawing:
sequence of building entry
elements.

（前頁、上）ロビー。
（前頁、下）アクソノメトリック図：ロビ
ーのつながり。
（上）アクソノメトリック図：ロビーを構
成するコンポーネント。

8 10   15   25

(above) Sectional perspective of
the lobby and Park Avenue
looking south.
Rendering by Richard Rochon.
(below, from left to right)
Floor plans: typical highrise
level; typical midrise level;
typical lowrise level; and
ground floor.

（上）ロビーの内部とパーク・アヴェニュ
ーを見た断面パース。南側を見る。
（下、左から右に）高層部基準階、中層部
基準階、低層部基準階、1階平面図。

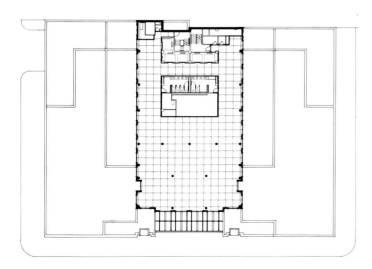

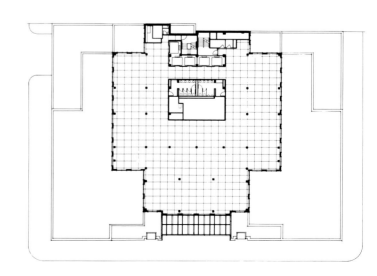

0 10 25 32 50

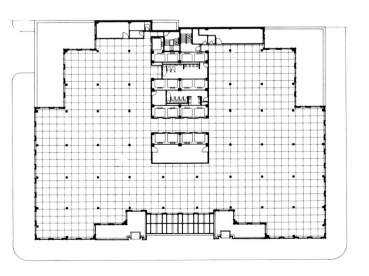

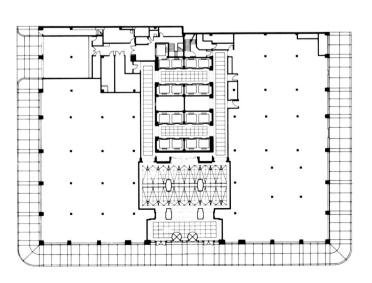

One Broadway Place
New York, New York

ワン・ブロードウェイ・プレイス
ニューヨーク州ニューヨーク

1989

One Broadway Place sits at the "bow-tie" intersection of Broadway and Seventh Avenue, the center of the Times Square district. The design of this 1,000,000-square-foot building resolves the challenges imposed by a set of complex zoning issues and an irregular site, while expressing the divergent characteristics of both retail and office uses.

Fronting on Broadway, a five-story retail atrium reflects the character and vibrancy of its Times Square location. The office entrance on 45th Street serves as an elegant transition to the office floors above. Connected by a block-through galleria, these two components function both individually and collectively.

The design of the building maximizes floor space while responding to strict zoning criteria. The tower is set back from Broadway to allow the "prow" of the building and its prominent steeple-like pinnacle, serving as point of exclamation, to step forward toward the street, reinforcing the "bow-tie" of the street grid below. Clad in monochromatic blue glass with flush mullions, a central vertical element anchors the corner and provides a distinctive presence. The 46th Street facade is clad in green glass, expressed silver mullions, and white spandrels, defining both the inner structural layer and the mass as an appendage to the central form. These distinct expressions create the impression of separate masses intersecting and enveloping one another.

ワン・ブロードウェイ・プレイスは、タイムズ・スクエア付近でブロードウェイと7番街が「蝶ネクタイ」のように交差する場所に位置する。9万3,000㎡の建物は、複雑なゾーニングや不規則な敷地に起因する難問を解決する役目を果たす。また、商業施設とオフィスそれぞれの利用者の異なった特性に見合うようになっている。

ブロードウェイに面する商業空間の5層分のアトリウムは、タイムズ・スクエアという場所柄の雰囲気、ざわめきを映し出す。45丁目側のオフィス・エントランスは、次の階にはじまるオフィス階へと滑らかにつづく。オフィス・エントランスとそれにつながる開放的なガレリアとで、個人用と団体用のいずれにも対応可能である。

建物は、厳密なゾーニングの基準に従って床面積を最大限に確保するように設計している。タワーは、ブロードウェイからセットバックし、「船首」のような端部とよく目立つ尖頭形の頂部が引き立って、眼下のグリッド状の街路の中で「蝶ネクタイ」を強調するように通りに面して足を踏みおろしている。

同一面のマリオンをもった青一色のガラスをまとって、中央の垂直のエレメントは建物のコーナーを引き締め、独特の存在感を出している。46丁目側のファサードは、銀色のマリオンと白色のスパンドレルで縁どられた緑色のガラスで覆われており、内部の構造材の層と、中央部に付随するマスとの境界を明確にしている。これらの異なった表現で、互いに干渉し合ったり別の部分を包み込んだりしているマスを分割した印象に見せている。　　　　(河野裕訳)

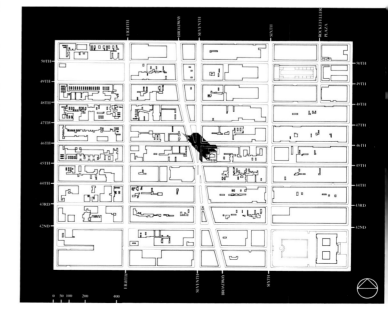

(right) Site plan.
(opposite) View of the south facade from the bow-tie intersections between Seventh Avenue and Broadway. Rendering by Richard Rochon.

(右)配置図。
(次頁)7番街とブロードウェイのつくる蝶ネクタイの交差点から見た南側ファサード。

(right) Exploded axonometric: retail base and advertising signage addresses Times Square; office component addresses 45th Street; spire marks this place in the city skyline.
(below) Context diagram: Tower and spire identify the "bow-tie" intersections that create Times Square.
(opposite) View from the northwest.
Photo by Wolfgang Hoyt.

（右）分解組立図：基部の店舗と広告板とがタイムズ・スクエアに、またオフィス部分が45丁目に対応する。尖塔はニューヨークのスカイラインにおけるこの場所を印象づける。

（下）コンテクスト・ダイアグラム：タワーと尖塔がタイムズ・スクエアを構成する蝶ネクタイの交差点を際立たせる。

（次頁）北西から見る。

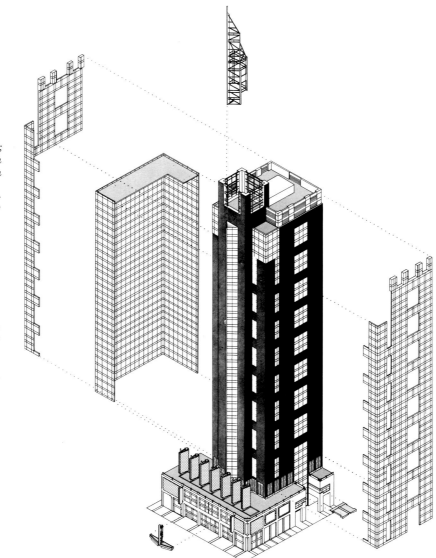

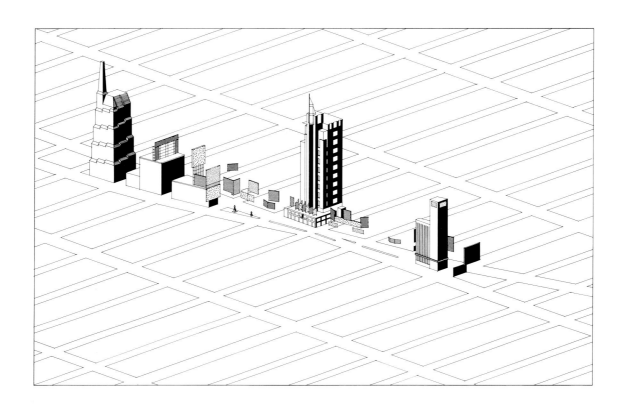

(right) Axonometric: top and
base of the building.
(opposite, left) West elevation.
(opposite, right) South elevation.

(右)アクソノメトリック図:基部と頂部。
(次頁、左)西側立面図。
(次頁、右)南側立面図。

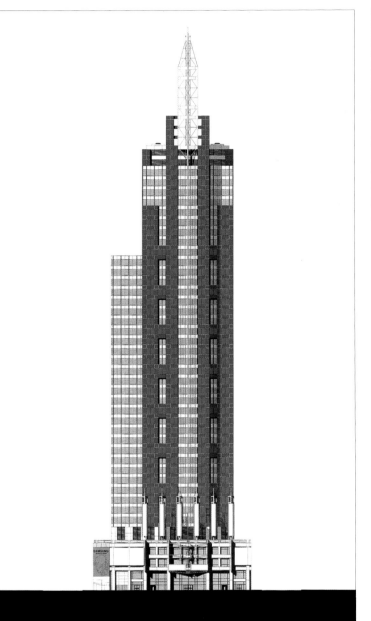

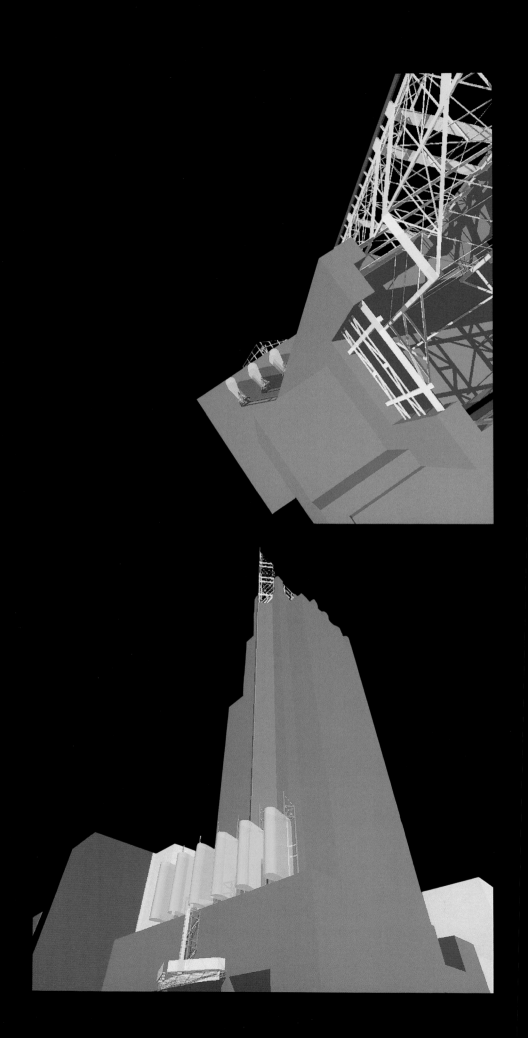

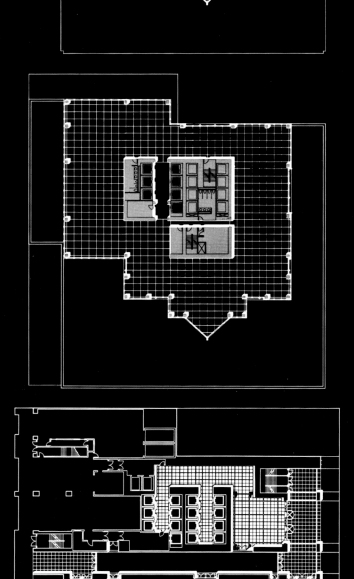

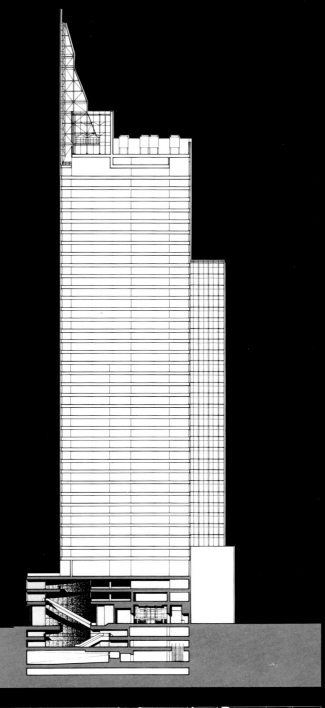

(top left) Section.
*(bottom left) Axonometric
drawing: lobby sequence.*

(左上)断面図。
(左下)アクソノメトリック図：オフィ
ス・ロビーのつながり。

0　16　32　48　64

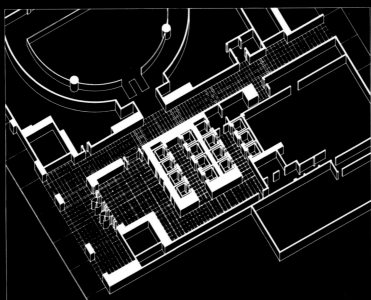

Madison Square Garden Site Redevelopment

New York, New York
in collaboration with Frank O. Gehry Associates
マディソン・スクエア・ガーデン
ニューヨーク州ニューヨーク
（フランク・ゲーリィとの共同設計）
1987

The design concept for the Madison Square Garden site creates an individual presence for each of three new office buildings while expressing a diversity of character to create an urban vitality for the site.

The three towers, dramatically distinct in form and rising from a common base, are joined by a "Great Hall" that lies beneath a glass roof that links Eighth Avenue with the private cross street at the center of the site. The Great Hall provides a place to gather as well as access to the upper level office lobbies of all three towers, the train and subway connections, and the proposed people mover. Each of these destinations also has a discrete entrance from the surrounding streets.

Terminating the Great Hall, Tower C provides a focus for the site, retaining the material of the base to provide a visual tie to Eighth Avenue. South of the Great Hall, Tower B is distinguished by curving elements front and rear and a rotated cube at its crown that animate the building mass and focus it skyward. Completing the composition of towers, to the north of the Great Hall, Tower A reads as a continuous shaft buttressed by larger floors at the lower levels. The core of the building is delineated at the exterior by the curving articulated glazing wall culminating in the intricate detail of the building's tiara, serving as a crown for not only Tower A but also the entire composition of towers.

コンセプトは、都市の活力を創出するために、三つの新しいオフィス・ビルディングにそれぞれ異なるキャラクターを与えることにより、各々の建物の存在感を創出することにある。

共通の基壇から立ち上がり、しかし形態において劇的に異なる3本の塔は、ガラスの屋根で覆われた「グレート・ホール」によって結びつけられている。また「グレート・ホール」は敷地中央を通る私道と8番街とを結び付けるものである。グレート・ホールは3本の塔の上層のオフィスのロビーへのアクセス動線としてだけではなく列車や地下鉄の連絡、そしてわれわれの提案した動く歩道の集中する場所としての機能も果たしている。また、これら各々の目的は周辺の街路からエントランスを分離させることにもある。

グレート・ホールの最奥部には、「タワーC」が焦点を与えている。タワーCの基壇の材質は8番街との視覚的結び付きを意識して選定されている。グレート・ホールの南には、前面と背面に湾曲面をもち、その頂部に軸を振った直方体を乗せた「タワーB」がそびえる。それらの要素は、建物に活力を与え、空への焦点を与える。グレート・ホールの北には3本の塔の構成を完成させるために、下層部において連続的な大構造のブレースの構成される「タワーA」がそびえる。頂部において複雑なディテールを描く王冠を擁するタワーAは円筒形のガラス・カーテンウォールによって明瞭に特徴づけられる。この王冠は、タワーAのみならず、この街区全体の塔の象徴としての役目を果たしている。

（高木義雄訳）

(right) Site plan.
(opposite) Aerial view. Empire State Building is visible at the back.
Rendering by Richard Rochon.

（右）配置図。
（次頁）空から見る。エンパイア・ステイト・ビルディングが後方に見える。

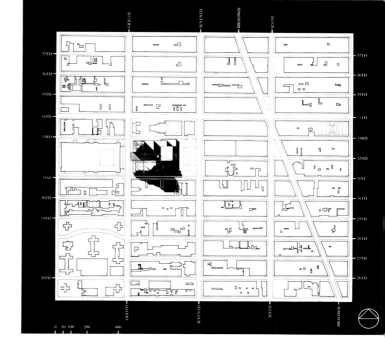

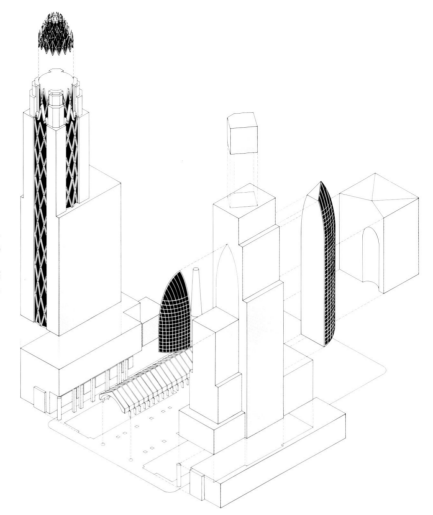

*(top right) Concept diagram:
contrast and dialogue between
the towers.
(bottom right) Context diagram:
relationship of tower to the
height, form, and articulation
of the Empire State Building.
(opposite) View from the
northwest.
Photo by Wolfgang Hoyt.*

(右上)コンセプト・ダイアグラム：ゲー
リィのタワーとチャイルズのタワーとの
対比と対話。
(右下)コンテクスト・ダイアグラム：高
さ、形態、分節についてエンパイア・ス
テイト・ビルディングと二つのタワーと
の関わり。
(次頁)北西から見る。

(above left) Two towers of
the Chartreuse Cathedral,
France.
(above right) Madison Square
Garden project with the gate
composed by two towers.
Photo by Wolfgang Hoyt.
(opposite) Axonometric drawing:
tops of the two towers.

(左上)フランスのシャルトル大聖堂の二
つの塔。
(右上)二つのタワーが門を形成するマデ
ィソン・スクエア・ガーデン計画。
(次頁)アクソノメトリック図：二つのタ
ワーの頂部。

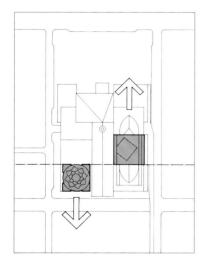

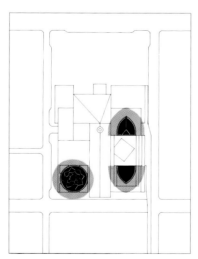

(above, from left to right)
Diagrams: tower locations;
insertion and attachment; and
attitudes of crowns. Building
offsets in dynamic juxtaposition
to maximize views and
emphasize contrast in form and
attitude.

(上、左から右に)ダイアグラム：タワー
の位置／挿入と付着／クラウンの形態と
方向性。二つのタワーが補完しあうダイ
ナミックな並置により、眺望を最大限に
確保し、形態とその姿の対比を強調する。

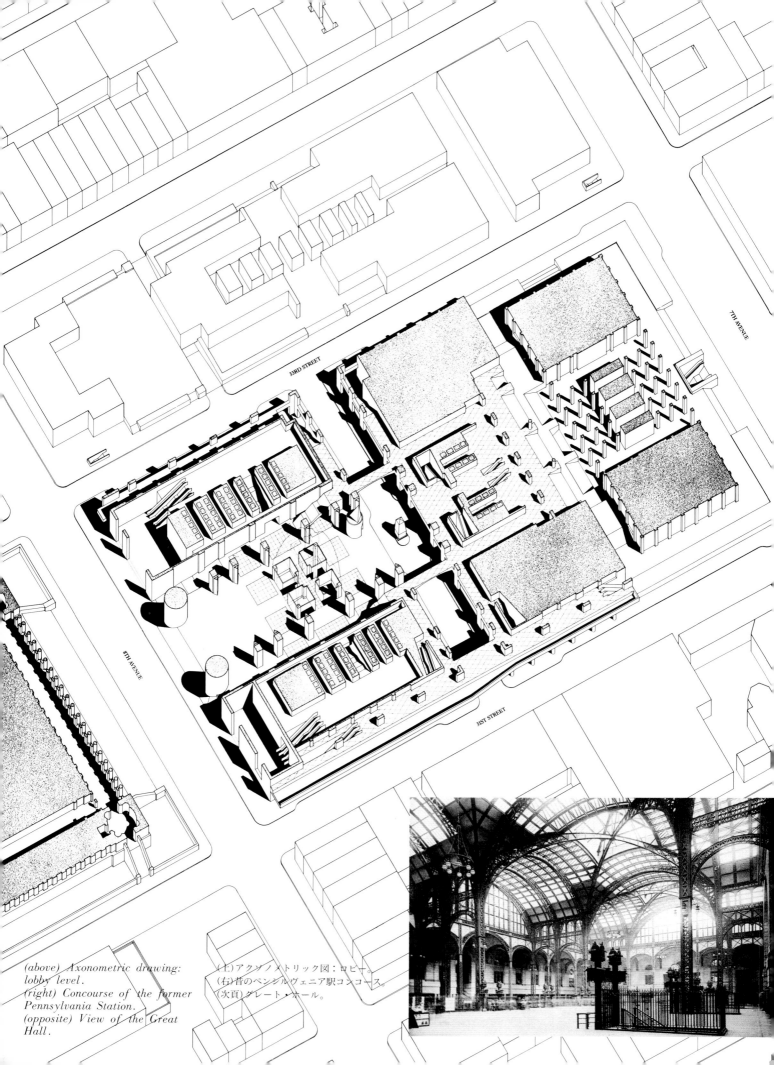

33RD STREET

7TH AVENUE

8TH AVENUE

31ST STREET

(above) Axonometric drawing:
lobby level.
(right) Concourse of the former
Pennsylvania Station.
(opposite) View of the Great
Hall.

（上）アクソノメトリック図：ロビー。
（右）昔のペンシルヴェニア駅コンコース。
（次頁）グレート・ホール。

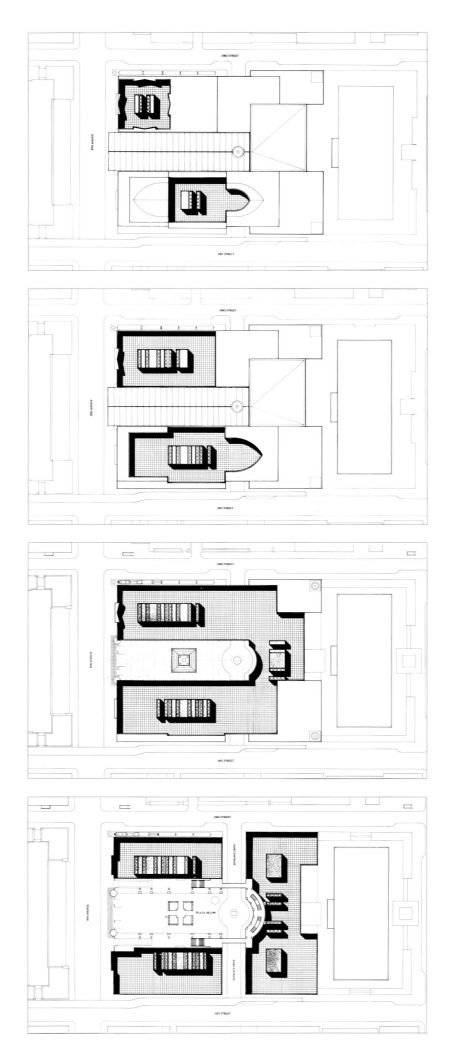

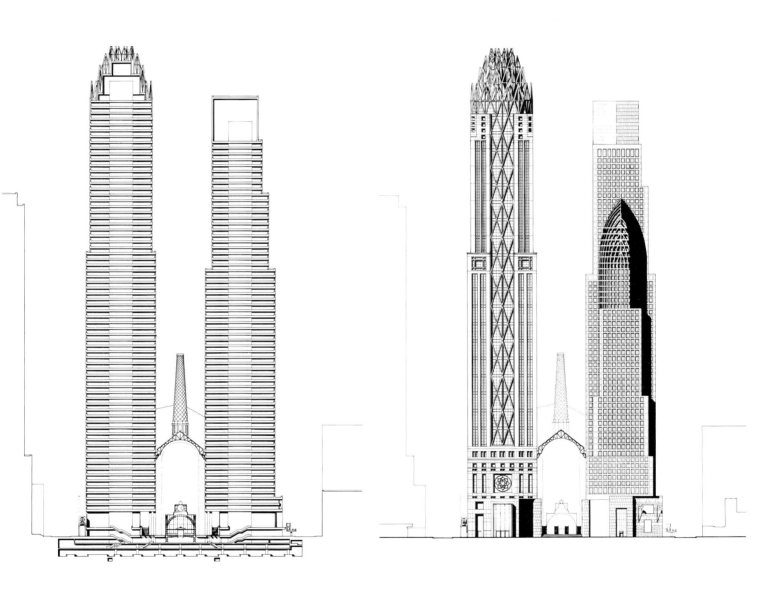

(opposite, from top to bottom)
Plans: high tower level; mid
tower level; low tower level;
base tower level.
(above left) Section.
(above right) Eighth Avenue
Elevation.

（前頁、上から下に）タワー平面図：
高層階。中層階。低層階。基部。
（左上）断面図。
（右上）8番街側立面図。

The Tribeca Pedestrian Bridge

New York, New York

トライベカ・ペデストリアン・ブリッジ
ニューヨーク州ニューヨーク

1992

The pedestrian bridge provides a safe, grade-separated crossing over the busy West Street/Route 9A corridor, connecting the new Stuyvesant High School to the esplanade and public open spaces of Battery Park City in Lower Manhattan. This civic structure serves a dual role, both as pedestrian circulation above and as a gateway for the vehicular traffic below.

The design of the structure specifically celebrates these culturally important functions in its composition, expressing the sense of the gateway by the spanning structure of two parallel bowstring trusses, offset from each other to reflect the street axis below. Pedestrian movement is emphasized by the glass and metal walkway enclosure, primarily composed of a series of horizontal elements that seem suspended within the structural system.

The towers, marking the east and west ends of the bridge, house the elevators, providing full access for all members of the community. The tops of these towers, entry canopies, and other details are constructed of stainless steel to provide ornamentation and focus at these key features. The eastern stair, constructed of cast-in-place concrete, curves around the elevator tower in the tradition of an inviting grand staircase. Furthering the sense of announcement, twin light columns are placed as newel posts at the base of the stairs. The stairs at the western terminus of the bridge, also detailed in stainless steel, provide egress for pedestrians not entering the school.

ニューヨーク、ロウア・マンハッタンのトライベカ・ペデストリアン・ブリッジは、交通量の多いウェスト・ストリート（ルート９Ａ通り）にたいする安全性を考え、それをまたぐかたちで立体交差し、スタイヴサント高等学校とバッテリィ・パーク・シティの遊歩道あるいは公共緑地とを結び付けている。この都市的な構造体は、それ自体が歩行者のための遊歩道であると同時に、下を通過する車にとってのゲートウェイの役割を果たす。

この構造体のデザインの特筆すべき点はその構成の中に文化的に重要な機能——二つの弓形トラスが、互いに平行に、かつ、下方の通りの軸に対応してそれぞれ支点をずらし、ゲートウェイとしての象徴性を高めている——をもっていることである。この構造システムの間に吊り下げられたように見える通路は、ガラスと金属で被われ、水平方向の要素の組合せで構成されており、歩行者の動きを力強く表現している。

橋の、東西それぞれの橋詰を示す塔は、エレヴェータを備え、地域のあらゆる人々を十分に迎え入れることができるようになっている。これらの塔の頂部、入口のキャノピィ、その他の部分のディテールは、ステンレス・スティールでつくられ、全体の基調の中で装飾的な役割をなしており、観る者の注意を引く。東詰の階段は、現場打ちのコンクリート製で、エレヴェータ塔に沿って曲線を描き、魅力的な大階段となっている。さらに、目印となるように最下段の両脇の親柱として照明塔が配置されている。橋の西端の階段もステンレス・スティールで詳細につくられており、学校側への入口というよりむしろ歩行者のための出口として機能する。

（河野裕訳）

(right) Site plan.
(opposite) View from Chambers Street on the south.
Rendering by Richard Rochon.

（右）配置図。
（次頁）南側のチャンバース通りから見る。

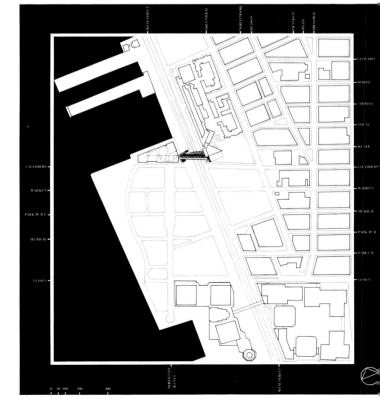

(right) Components of the bridge: access and passage.
(below) View of the bridge crossing over West Street from the west.
Photo by Bryan Nolan.

(右)橋のコンポーネント：橋詰と橋上。
(下)ウェスト・ストリートに架かる橋を西から見る。

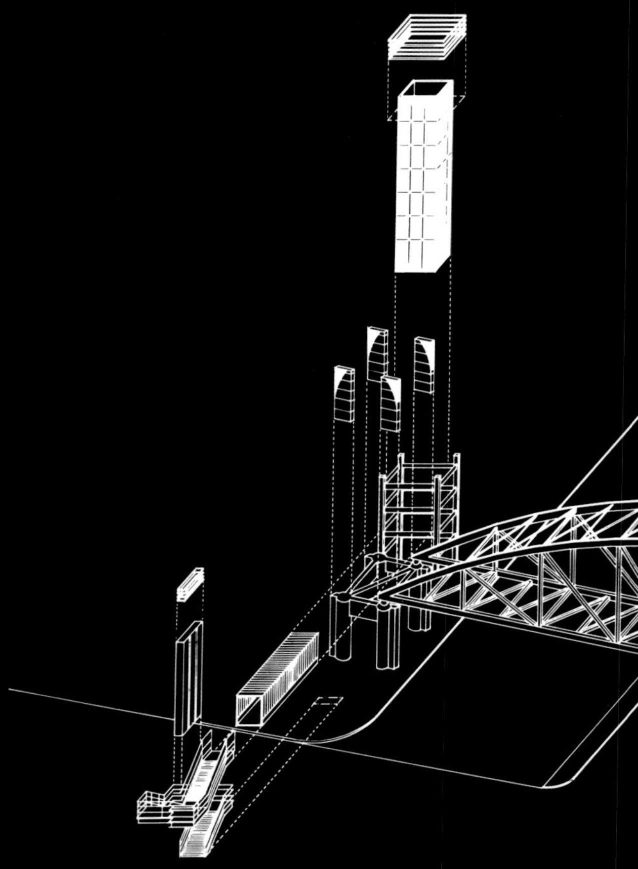

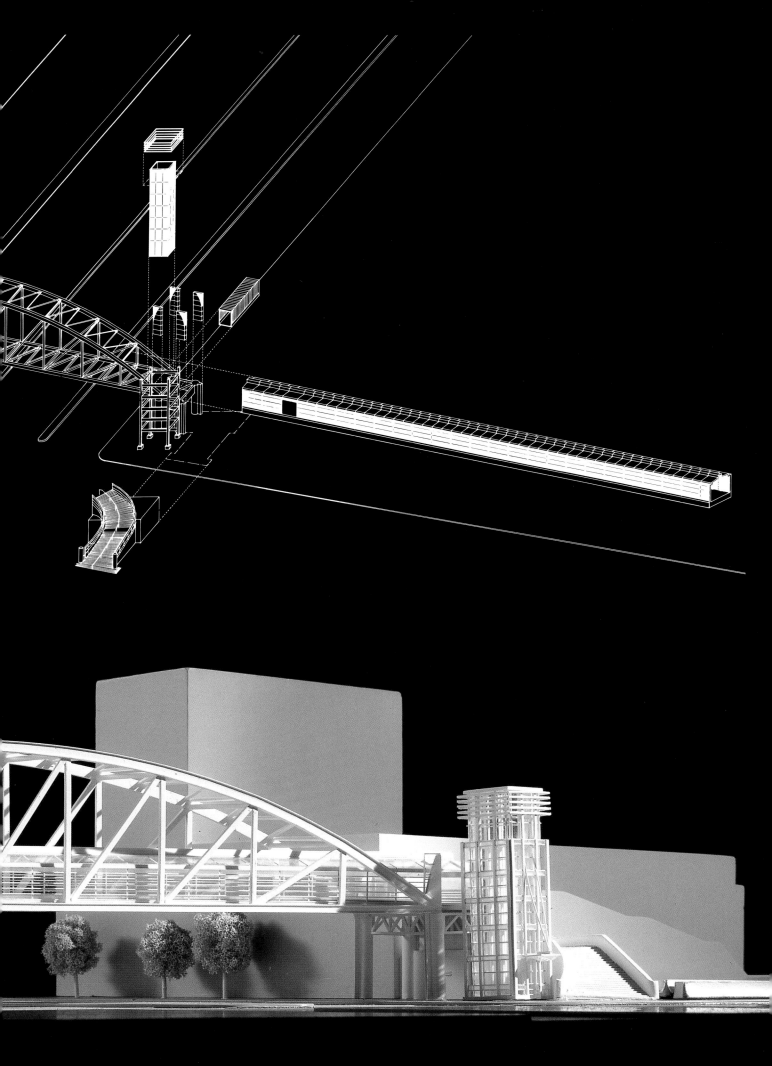

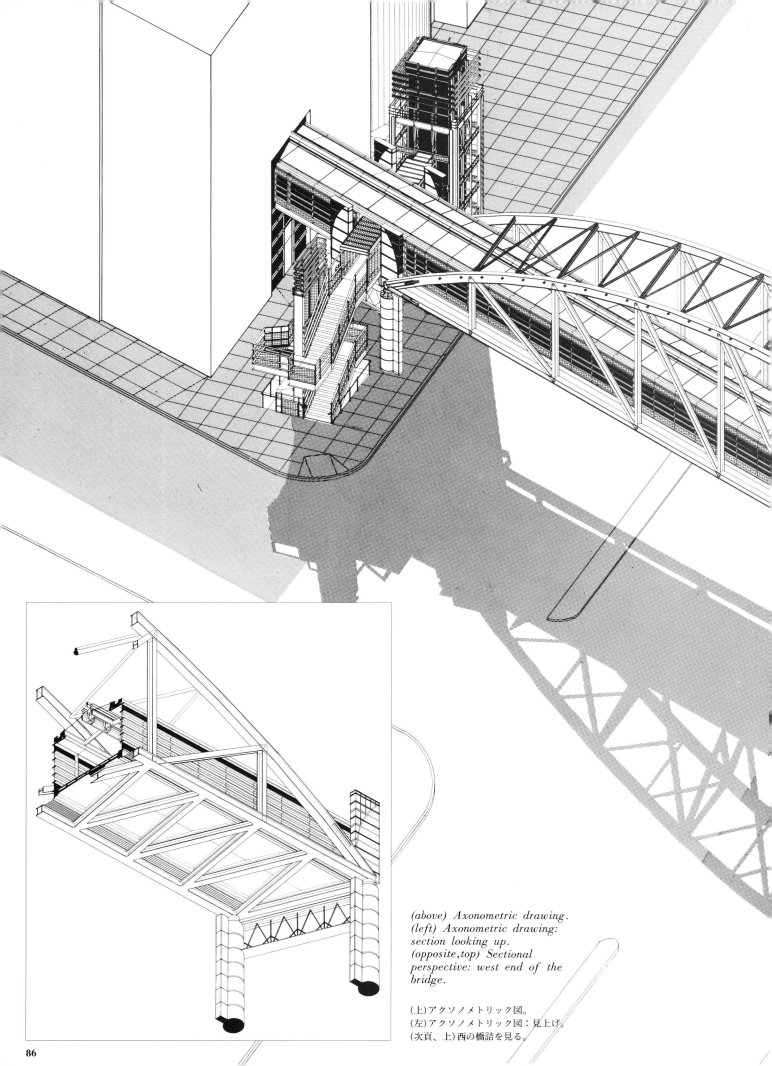

(above) Axonometric drawing.
(left) Axonometric drawing:
section looking up.
(opposite,top) Sectional
perspective: west end of the
bridge.

(上)アクソノメトリック図。
(左)アクソノメトリック図：見上げ。
(次頁、上)西の橋詰を見る。

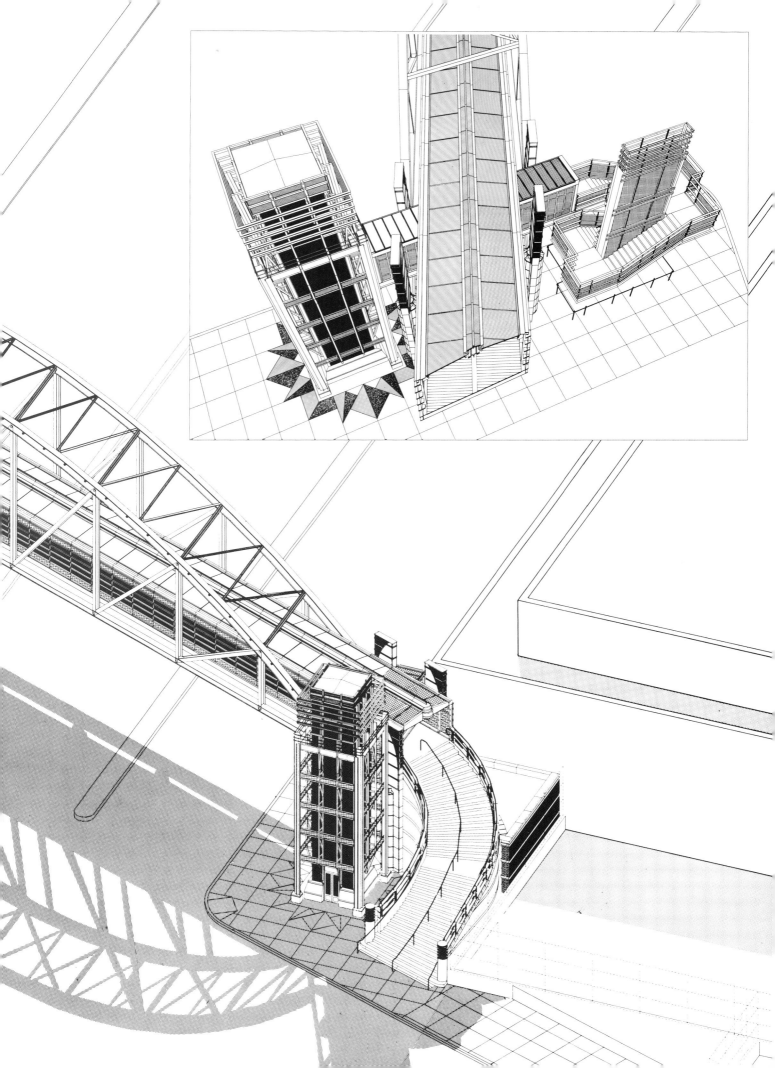

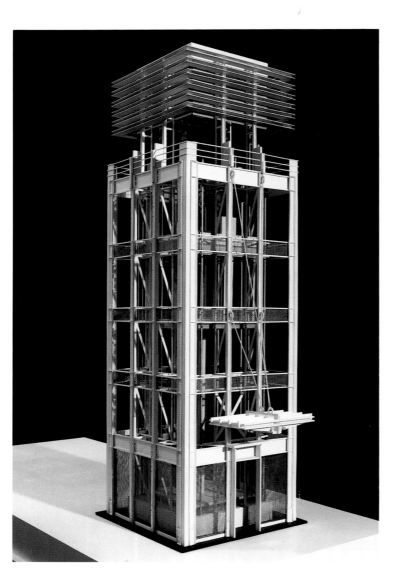

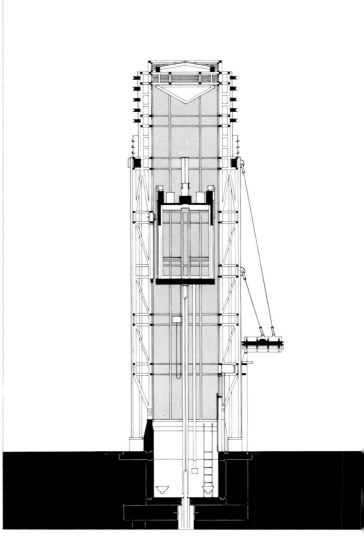

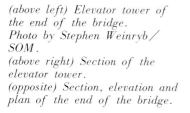

(above left) Elevator tower of the end of the bridge. Photo by Stephen Weinryb/ SOM.
(above right) Section of the elevator tower.
(opposite) Section, elevation and plan of the end of the bridge.

（左上）橋詰のエレヴェータ・タワー。
（右上）エレヴェータ・タワー断面図。
（次頁）橋詰の断面図、立面図、平面図。

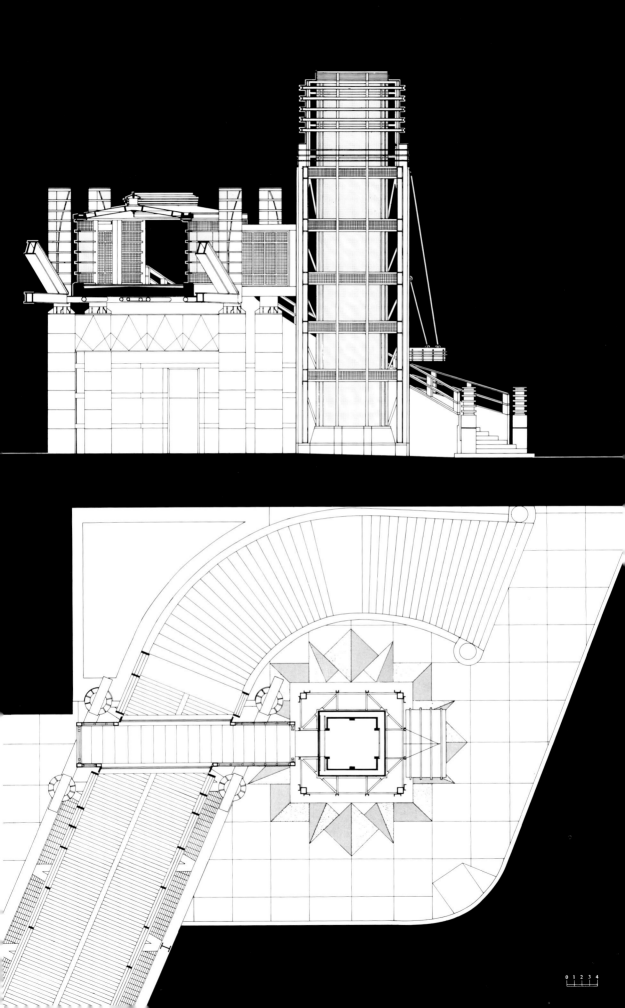

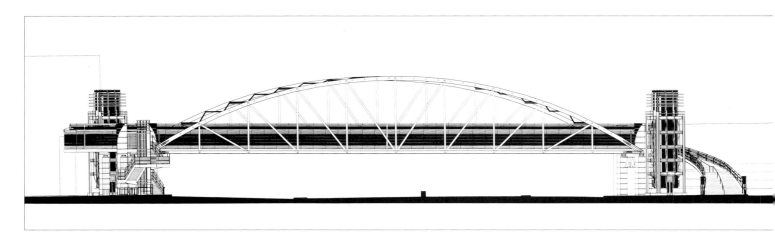

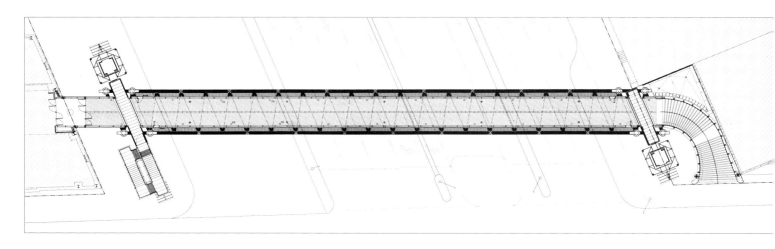

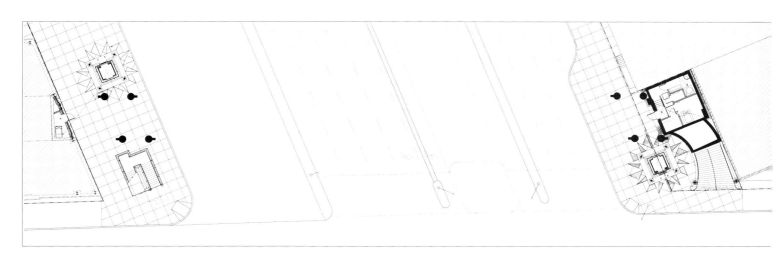

(top) South elevation.
(middle) Walkway level plan.
(above) Street level plan.
(opposite) Aerial view.
Photo by Stephen Weinryb/
SOM.

(上)南側立面図。
(中)歩行路平面図。
(下)ストリート・レヴェル平面図。
(次頁)真上から見たトライベカ・ブリッジ。

Built Projects

450 Lexington Avenue
New York, New York

450 レキシントン・アヴェニュー
ニューヨーク州ニューヨーク

1992

450 Lexington Avenue is a 40-story office tower addition to the historic Grand Central Station Post Office. The design solved the structural intricacies of locating footings between the railroad tracks of Grand Central Station, while maintaining the spirit of the landmark building that serves as the tower's base. The building establishes a strong presence on an important Midtown site while remaining consistent with the details of its historic base.

In this constricted commercial district, the full height of the project is rarely, if ever, seen as a whole. To consolidate the glimpses of the building one sees from the street, neighboring buildings, and distant angles, a consistent building theme of rotated-square decorative elements taken from the Post Office's facade was incorporated throughout the building, culminating in a crowning "basket" of metal and glass at the top of the tower. This crown, illuminated from within at night, marks 450 Lexington's image among the historic buildings within this portion of Manhattan's skyline.

Access to the office floors is through a processional sequence of spaces rarely seen in New York, beginning with the existing structure's monumental portals serving as ground floor entrance lobbies. Shuttle elevators transfer tenants to the sixth-floor *piano nobile* "sky lobby", a grand double-height space overlooking terrace gardens.

450 レキシントン・アヴェニューは、グランド・セントラル駅郵便局の歴史的な建物に、40層のオフィス・タワーを加えるものである。駅の線路をまたぐ基礎部分の構造の複雑さを解決するデザインがなされ、駅自体は、タワーの基壇として機能しつづける。この建物は、ミッドタウンの重要な場所において、歴史的基盤のもつ細やかさを調和しながらも強烈な存在感を打ち出す。

この商業地区の高さ制限いっぱいに建てられるプロジェクトはほとんどなく、あるにしてもきわめて稀で、全体として統一された高さが保たれている。通りから、あるいは隣りの建物や別の角度からこの建物を一目見たときに周囲との一体感が得られるように、郵便局のファサードから引用した四周飾りの要素といった題材が一貫して建物の至るところに組み込まれていて、金属とガラスでできた頂部の「かご」へと達している。この頂部は、夜間には内部から照らされることにより、マンハッタンのスカイラインの一部を構成する歴史的な建物群の中での450レキシントンのイメージをより特徴あるものとしている。

1階部分のエントランス・ロビーとして機能する既存部分の正門を起点に、ニューヨークでは滅多に見られない列状の空間を通り抜け、オフィス階へとアクセスする。シャトル・エレヴェータは、人々を6階の「スカイ・ロビー」へと案内する。そこは、ピアノ・ノービレ(主階)であり、テラス・ガーデンを見渡すことのできる巨大な2層吹抜けの空間となっている。　　　　　(河野裕訳)

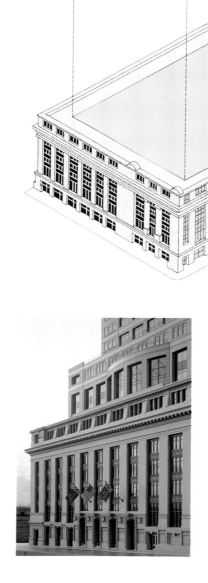

(top right) Axonometric drawing. (bottom right) View of the existing Grand Central Station Post Office as the tower's base. (opposite) View from the northeast. Chrysler Building and PANAM Building are visible. Photos (pp.94-95) by Joe Aker.

(右上)アクソノメトリック図。
(右下)タワーの基部となる歴史的建築グランド・セントラル駅郵便局を見る。
(次頁)北東から見る。クライスラー・ビルとパンナム・ビルが見える。

(top left) Skylobby.
(bottom left) Ground floor lobby.
Photos (p.96) by Wolfgang Hoy
(opposite, left from top to bottom Typical floor plan; skylobby floor plan; ground floor plan.
(opposite, top right) Site plan.
(opposite, bottom right) Section.

（左上）スカイロビー。
（左下）1階ロビー。
（次頁、左上から左下に）
基準階平面図。スカイロビー階平面図。
1階平面図。
（次頁、右上）配置図。
（次頁、右下）断面図。

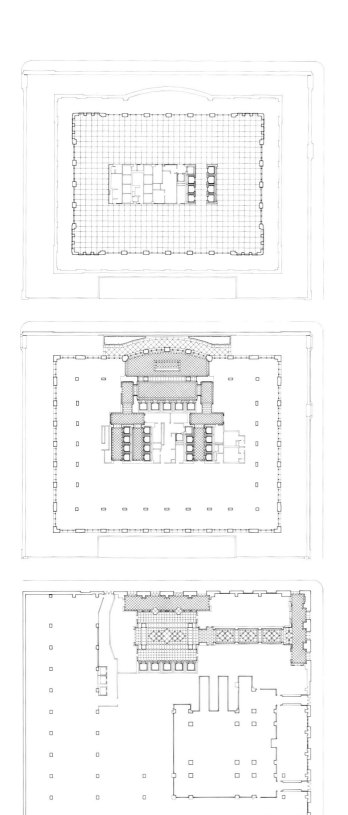

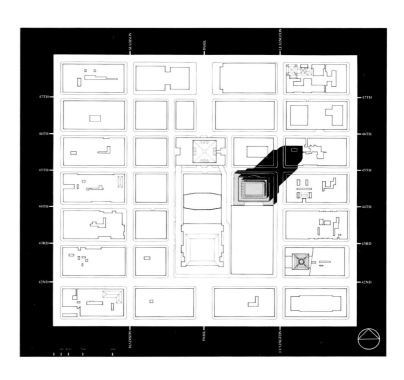

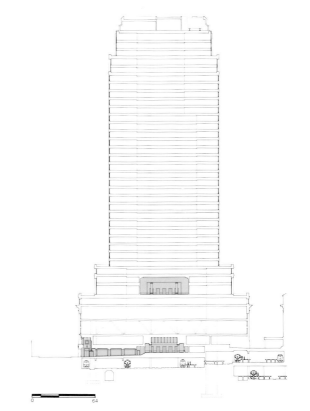

255 Fifth Street

Cincinnati, Ohio

255 フィフス・ストリート
オハイオ州シンシナティ

1990

Rising 30 stories into the Cincinnati skyline, 255 Fifth Street is a 450,000-square-foot structure expressed through a succession of setbacks that define and accentuate the building's base, middle, and top. The base, containing the lobby, a two-story loggia, retail shops, and carefully concealed parking, reflects the cornice line of an adjoining neo-classical theater and reinforces the scale of neighboring buildings. As a virtual extension of the plaza located diagonally across Fifth Street, the loggia also assumes the characteristics of a grand public space.

Sited mid-block to preserve views from existing buildings, the tower rises from the articulated base, culminating in a final series of setbacks that define the building's top. Notched window bays and continuous granite pilasters emphasize the verticality of the building as it reaches towards its crown. The crown is accentuated by a series of "jewels," defined by illuminated, rotated-square accent stones framed within granite recesses. These "jewels" are bathed in a seasonal change of color, establishing 255 Fifth Street as a dynamic contributor to the annual festival of lights and the city's exuberant skyline.

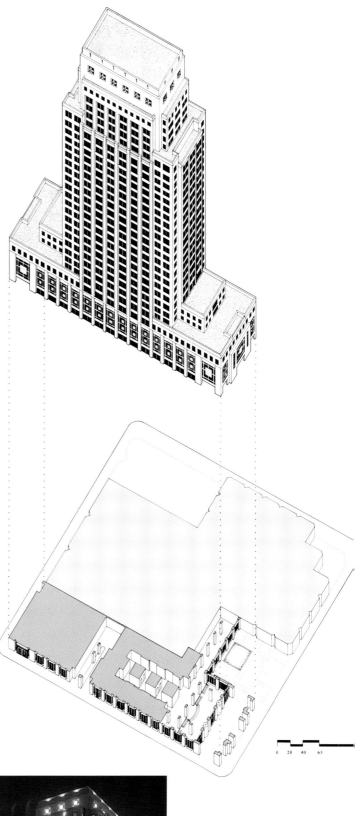

シンシナティの空へ向けて30層4万2,000m²の255フィフス・ストリートは、連続するセットバックによりビルの基壇と中層、頂部が特徴づけられている。建物の基壇部分にはロビー、2層吹抜けのロッジア（外部廊下）、小売店舗そして注意深く隠された駐車場が計画されている。そしてその基壇は隣接する新古典主義の劇場とコーニスの位置を揃え、近隣のスケールに合わせるよう気を使っている。また、フィフス・ストリートをはさんで向かいに位置する広場にロッジアを面することによって、地上レヴェルの公共空間の表情にたいしても貢献をしている。街区の中央部に位置するこの建物は、周囲の既存の建物群により眺望を妨げられないよう基壇部とは明瞭に区別されたタワーが、頂部に至るまで連続するセットバックにより、構成される。柱ごとにきざまれる出窓と、縦に通る花崗岩の柱形は頂部に向かって、建物の垂直性を強調する。建物の頂部は柱ごとに置かれた「宝石」によりアクセントをつけている。それは花崗岩の壁面のくぼみにはめこまれ、軸を回転させながら照明により映しだされる立方体のアクセントの石である。この「宝石」は都市の華麗なスカイラインや年に一度の光の祭典への重要な貢献者としての255フィフス・ストリートの存在を確立し、季節の移り変わりに応じて、様々な色を反映するのである。

（高木義雄訳）

(top right) Axonometric drawing.
(bottom right) Night view of the upper part of 255 Fifth Street.
(opposite) View from the plaza on the northeast.
Photos (pp.98-99) by Robert Ames Cook.

（右上）アクソノメトリック図。
（右下）255フィフス・ストリートの上層部夜景。
（次頁）北東側にあるプラザから見る。

(top right) Site plan.
(bottom left) Ground floor plan.
(bottom right) Typical lowrise level plan.
(opposite) Night view of the exterior of the entrance.
Photo by Joe Aker.

(右上)配置図。
(左下)1階平面図。
(右下)低層階基準階平面図。
(次頁)メイン・エントランス外観夜景。

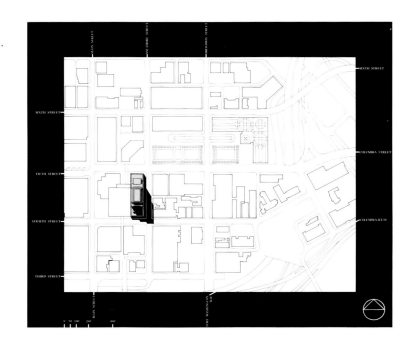

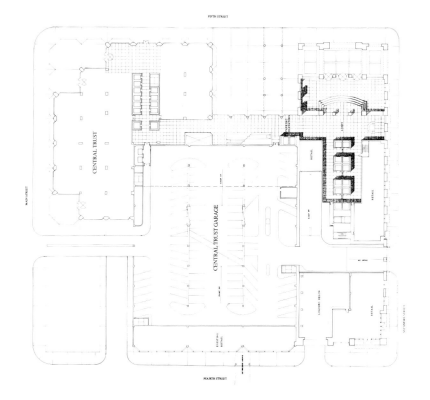

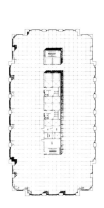

Worldwide Plaza

New York, New York

ワールドワイド・プラザ
ニューヨーク州ニューヨーク

1986

Worldwide Plaza, a mixed-use development encompassing an entire city block on the site of the former Madison Square Garden, reflects the transition from the higher density, commercial sector to the east and the smaller scale of the residential neighborhood of Clinton to the west. At the eastern end, a 47-story commercial office tower marks the site, while a complex of low, residential buildings defines the site to the west, and a mid-block residential tower mediates between the two. The adjoining plaza, a lively landscaped space, serves not only as a break in the 800-foot long block but also as a place of gathering for office workers and residents of both the development and the surrounding neighborhood.

The Eighth Avenue tower, containing approximately 1.5 million square feet, provides separate entries and identities for three lead tenants. The building, reflecting the heritage of traditional New York skyscrapers, is clad in stone and brick with clear glass windows and topped by a copper-clad pyramidal crown punctuated by round dormers. Set into the top of the crown is a glass prism, which when lit serves as a beacon for the entire West Side.

ワールドワイド・プラザは、かつてマディソン・スクエア・ガーデンのあった街区全体を取り囲む開発で、東へ伸びる高密度の商業地区と、西へ伸びるクリントンの小規模な住宅地区の変化に対応したものである。47層の商業オフィス棟が敷地の東側の境界を示して建ち、一方、低層の住居棟は西側の境界を示している。その中間部に、双方を結びつけるように住居棟が建っている。これに、鮮やかにランドスケープされたプラザが加わって、およそ245mの長い区画を分節すると同時に、オフィス・ワーカーと住民との交流の場所を提供している。

8番街のタワーは、面積が約14万㎡で、三つのテナントそれぞれに別の入口がある。伝統的なニューヨークのスカイスクレイパーを踏襲して、透明ガラス窓をもち、石や煉瓦で仕上げられ、頂部に銅で覆われたピラミッド状の冠がある。冠の先端は、ガラスのプリズムで、これが輝やいてウェスト・サイド全体の立標となる。

(河野裕訳)

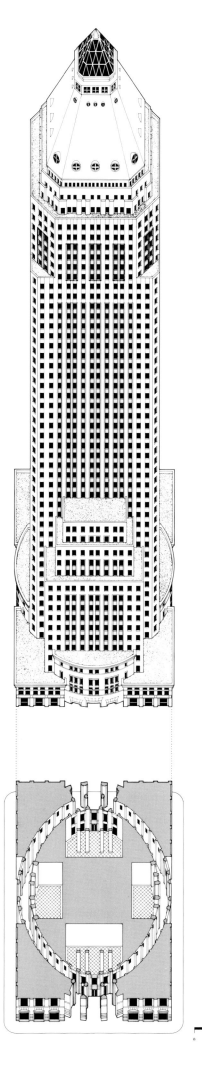

(right) Axonometric drawing.
(opposite) View of residential tower in the front and commercial office tower at the back from the northwest.
Photo by Addison Thompson.

(右)アクソノメトリック図。
(次頁)北西から見る。手前に住居棟、その後ろに商業オフィス棟が見える。

0 32 64 128 25

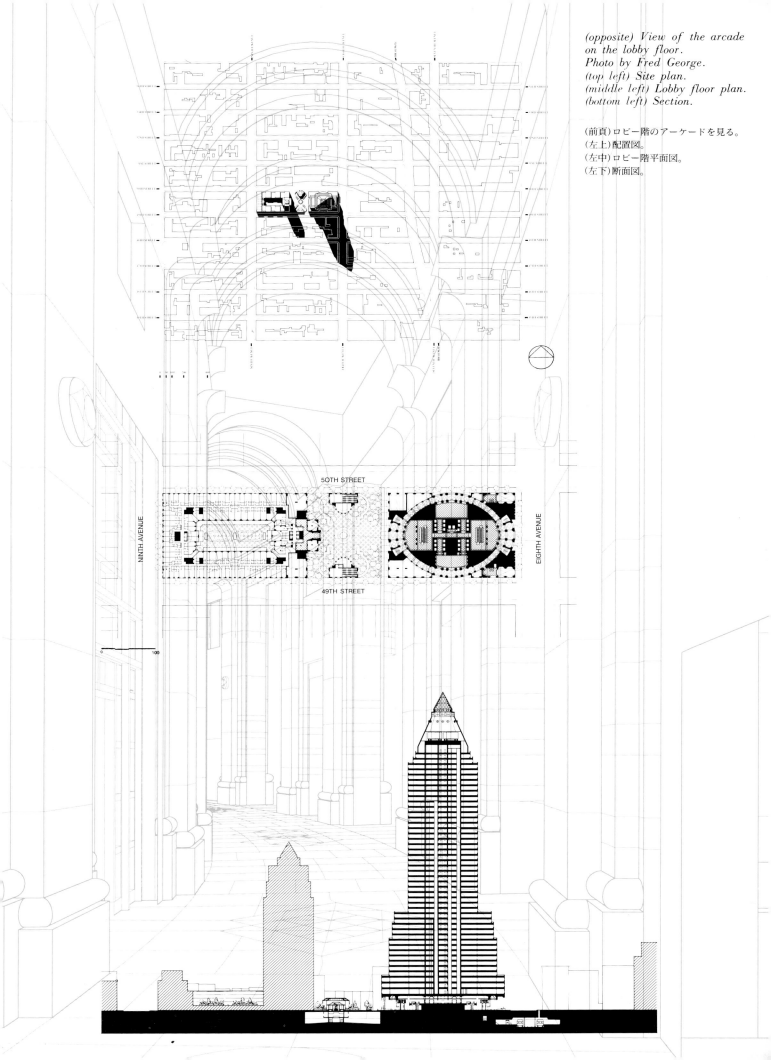

(opposite) View of the arcade
on the lobby floor.
Photo by Fred George.
(top left) Site plan.
(middle left) Lobby floor plan.
(bottom left) Section.

(前頁)ロビー階のアーケードを見る。
(左上)配置図。
(左中)ロビー階平面図。
(左下)断面図。

50TH STREET

NINTH AVENUE

EIGHTH AVENUE

49TH STREET

0   100

The U.S. News and World Report Complex

Washington, DC

US ニューズ・アンド・ワールド・レポート・コンプレックス

ワシントンDC

1991

The U.S. News and World Report Complex is located in an area of Washington that serves as a transition between the buildings of the governmental core, typically constructed of grey stone, and the residentially influenced structures of Georgetown, generally built of red brick. The complex expresses this transition through the blending of the scale, proportion and most particularly the materials typical to each of these two districts. Rosy oversized sand-molded brick reflects the Georgetown area while white buff cast-stone ribbons represent central Washington.

In the U.S. News and World Report Headquarters, variations in the horizontal banding combine with window recesses to define a base and crown. Providing emphasis and delineation for the entry, the assertive housing for the mechanical penthouse is balanced by a glass covered portico following the arc of the vehicular drop-off. Within the eight-story building, a four-story lobby concentrically follows the curve of the entry facade, allowing interior balconies a view to the reception area below or to the parkland beyond the mullioned curtain wall.

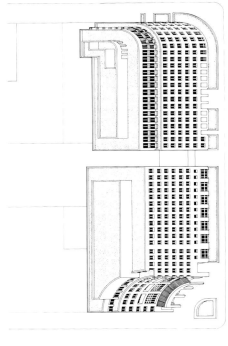

US ニューズ・コンプレックスは、ワシントンの中でも、灰色の石でつくられた典型的な官庁建築群と、大部分赤煉瓦造でジョージタウンの構法の影響を受けている住居群との間にあって、その転調の役割を果たす地区に位置している。この複合施設は、これら二つの地区に特有のスケール、プロポーション、とりわけ素材の混成のもたらす変化の様子を表現している。

赤みを帯びた大きすぎるくらいの煉瓦（砂の鋳型でつくられた）が、ジョージタウン地区の建物の特徴であるように、白みがかった淡黄色の人造石の帯は、セントラル・ワシントンの建物の特徴である。

US ニューズ・コンプレックスでは、くぼんだ窓が組み合わさって様々な水平の帯が形成され、基壇と頂部を分けている。エントランス部分を強調し、輪郭をはっきりさせることで、塔屋機械室とガラスで覆われたポルティコ（車寄せの円弧状の部分へと連らなる）とは釣り合いがとれている。8層のうち、4層分のロビーが入口側のファサードの円弧の部分に同心円状につながっていることで、内側のバルコニーからは下方にレセプション・エリア、そしてカーテンウォールのマリオン越しに公園を眺めることができる。　　　　　（河野裕訳）

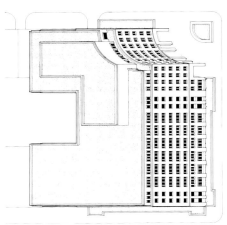

(right) Axonometric drawing.
(opposite) View towards the southwest from the intersection of 24th Street and N Street. Photo by Dan Cunningham.

（右）アクソノメトリック図。
（次頁）24丁目とNストリートの交差点から見る。

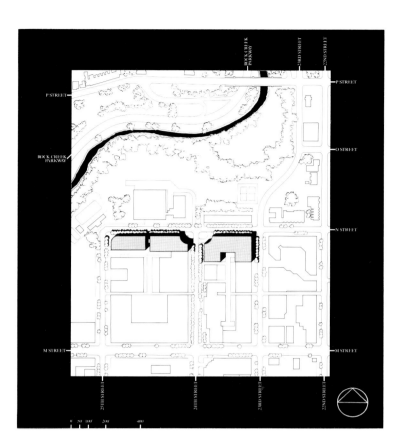

(opposite) Lobby.
Photo by Maxwell MacKenzie.
(top left) Site plan.
(middle left) Upper level plan.
(bottom left) Ground floor plan.

（前頁）ロビー。
（左上）配置図。
（左中）上層階平面図。
（左下）1階平面図。

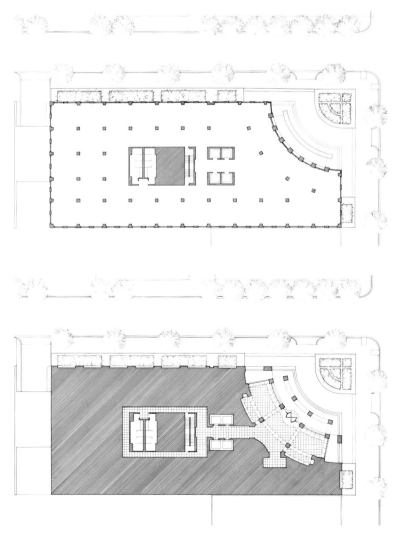

Evening Star

Washington, DC

イヴニング・スター
ワシントンDC

1990

The reuse and expansion of the historic 1898 Evening Star Building and its 1922 annex are important contributions to the revitalization of Pennsylvania Avenue, the nation's main street, which connects the U.S. Capitol Building with the White House. Given its historic character and its location across the avenue from the landmark Old Post Office and Tower, the Evening Star Building is part of an important building composition that forms a visual gateway to the public spaces to the west.

The Evening Star's facade was restored to its original design, and complemented by a new limestone addition that continues the proportional system of the earlier building, carrying through important horizontal divisions of the facade. Additional classical motifs, including balconies and pediments, strengthen the addition's relationship to the historic building without mimicking it.

1898年に建てられたイヴニング・スター・ビルならびに1922年のその増築部分の再利用と拡張計画は、ホワイト・ハウスをはじめとする合衆国の首府の建物を結び付けているこの国の重要な通り、ペンシルヴェニア・アヴェニューの再構成に寄与する重要なものである。イヴニング・スター・ビルは、その歴史的な特徴もさることながら、ランドマーク的な建物である旧郵便局とタワーにたいして通りをはさんだ位置にあるということで、重要な街区構成の一部を担い、西側の公共空間にたいして視覚的なゲートウェイとして機能するものである。

イヴニング・スターのファサードは、オリジナルのデザインに復元されているが、当時の建物に用いられた比例の構成手法にもとづいて水平方向に分割され、新しい石灰石の増築部分がこれを補足している。バルコニーやペディメントを含めて、古典的なモティーフを付加することで、模倣することなく歴史的な建物との関係がより強められる。 (河野裕訳)

(right) Axonometric drawing.
(bottom right) Axonometric diagram.
(opposite) View from the intersection of 11th Street and Pennsylvania Avenue.
Photos (p.111 and p.113) by Carol Peerce.

(右)アクソノメトリック図。
(右下)アクソノメトリック・ダイアグラム。
(次頁)11丁目とペンシルヴェニア・アヴェニューとの交差点から見る。

(top right) Site plan.
(middle right) Ground floor plan.
(bottom right) Section.
(below) South elevation.
(opposite) View of the lobby.

(右上)配置図。
(右中)1階平面図。
(右下)断面図。
(下)南側立面図。
(次頁)ロビー。

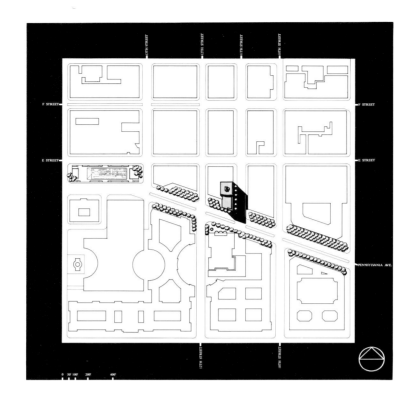

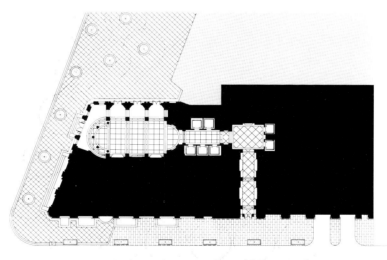

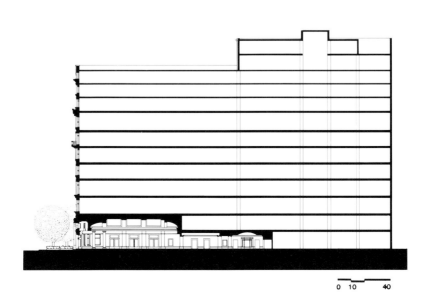

Providence Intercity Rail Station

Providence, Rhode Island

プロヴィデンス・ステーション
ロードアイランド州プロヴィデンス

1985

This new railroad station serves as the catalyst for an extensive urban development plan for downtown Providence, Rhode Island. The station relates to, but does not compete with, the adjacent State House designed by McKim, Mead, and White at the turn of the century. A dome over the main concourse and waiting area resolves the conflicting geometry between the interior spaces and exterior walls, giving the station a classical richness and civic presence. The clock tower, a traditional element of railroad station architecture, reinforces orientation and enhances the identity of the station.

この都市間鉄道駅の計画は、プロヴィデンスのダウンタウンの広範囲にわたる開発の触媒としての役割を果たすものである。この駅は近接する、今世紀初頭にマッキム、ミード・アンド・ホワイトにより設計されたステイト・ハウスと関係づけられるものであり、それと競い合うものではない。

メイン・コンコースおよび待合スペースの上部に架けられているドームは内部の空間と外部の壁面との幾何学的な接点を調停する。ドームはステイト・ハウスと同種の歴史的空間の豊穣さと都市の現在性を醸しだすものである。また鉄道駅建築の伝統的な要素である時計塔は、駅にたいする方向性を強調し、駅のアイデンティティを高めるものである。

この建築の壁面は石灰石により、また楣および柱はコンクリートにより構成されており、ドームはステンレス・スティールにより仕上げられている。駐車場は駅の入口広場の地下2階の部分に設けられている。 (高木義雄訳)

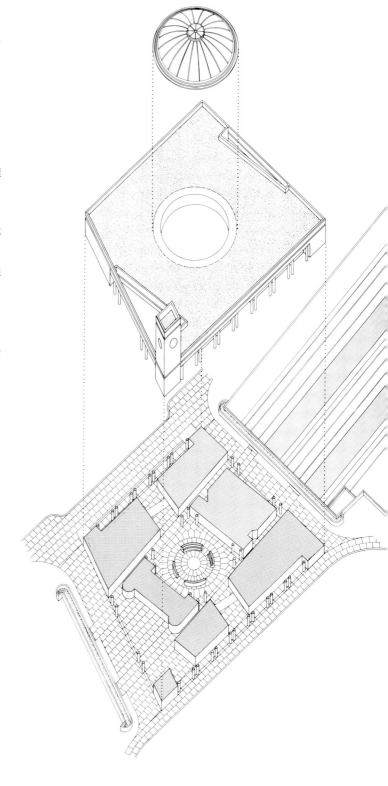

(right) Axonometric drawing.
(opposite) View from the northwest.
In the front, State House is visible.
Photo by Douglas Dalton.

(右)アクソノメトリック図。
(次頁)北西から見る。手前にステイト・ハウスが見える。

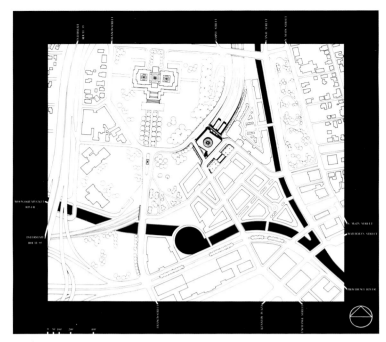

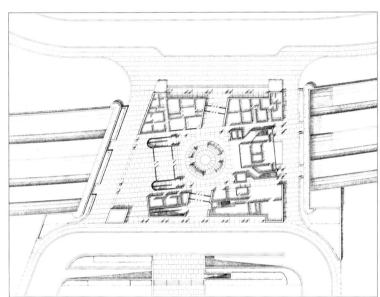

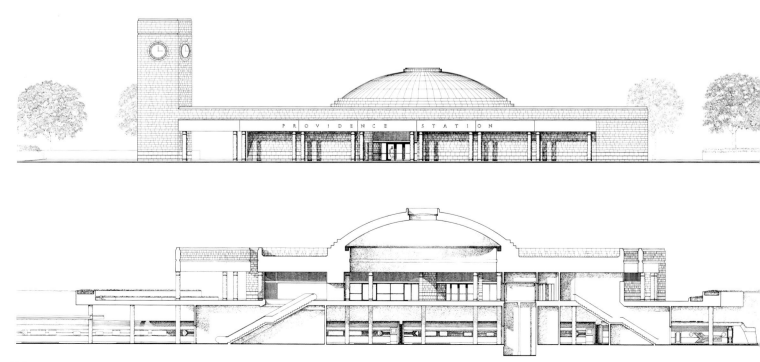

(opposite, from top to bottom)
Site plan.
Ground floor plan.
South elevation.
Section.
(above) View from the south.
Photo by Steve Rosenthal.

(前頁、上から下に)
配置図。
1階平面図。
南側立面図。
断面図。
(上)南側から見る。

1300 New York Avenue

Washington, DC

1300 ニューヨーク・アヴェニュー
ワシントンDC

1984

1300 New York Avenue, a one-million-square-foot structure with twelve floors above grade and four below, is the largest non-governmental office building in Washington, DC. Located on the approach to the White House, the building responds to the site's shallowly angled edge at the avenue's intersection with H Street, with a sweeping articulated facade expressing neoclassical architectural tradition. The curved center section is delineated by a series of punched-window recesses, overlaid by a four-story monumental arch, flanked by a smaller arch on either side, marking the principal entry. Anchored by solid end pieces punctuated with punched windows, the elements on either side of the entry contain paired columns supporting projecting beams to form a structural grid in front of the window wall. This tripartite theme also extends to the organization of horizontal elements: a monumental three-story limestone and granite base; a colonnaded buff precast midsection; and an ornamental cornice highlighted with tan masonry and buff concrete window surrounds. Crowning the building is a metal mansard roof, painted trilage green to echo the copper roofs of neighboring neoclassical structures and to contrast with the red metal roof of the adjacent landmark Masonic Temple.

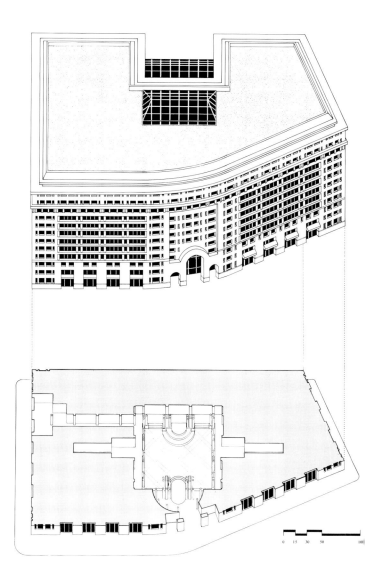

1300 ニューヨーク・アヴェニューは、面積が9万3,000㎡、地上12階、地下4階の建物で、ワシントンDCの民間のオフィス・ビルの中では最大級である。ホワイト・ハウスへの往路、新古典主義建築の伝統を明確に表現したファサードが連なるHストリートの交差点で、ゆるやかに角をなす敷地に沿って建っている。湾曲した中央部分の外観は、奥まって嵌め込まれた窓と、主玄関をなす4層分のモニュメンタルなアーチとその両脇のアーチとによって構成されている。入口にたいして両側のファサードでは、突き出した梁とそれを支える対になった柱は、窓間にエンドピースで固定され、ウィンドウ・ウォールの前面のグリッドを形成する。この三部構成による旋律は、垂直方向の要素にまで広がっている。すなわち、花崗岩と大理石で仕上げられたモニュメンタルな3層分の基壇、淡黄色のプレキャストの柱が並ぶ中層部、黄褐色の煉瓦と淡黄色のコンクリートによって際立つ装飾的な廻縁に表われている。建物の頂部は、隣接する新古典主義の建物の銅製の屋根に対応して緑銅色に塗られたマンサード屋根となっていて、近くのランドマーク的建造物であるフリーメーソン寺院の赤い金属屋根と対比をなしている。

(河野裕訳)

(top right) Axonometric drawing.
(bottom right) North elevation.
(opposite) View of the facade to New York Avenue.
Photo by Maxwell MacKenzie.

(右上)アクソノメトリック図。
(右下)北側立面図。
(次頁)ニューヨーク・アヴェニュー側のファサードを見る。

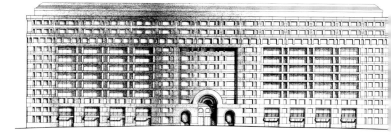

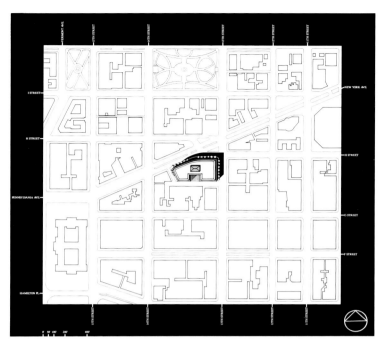

(opposite) View of the atrium lighted by the openings on the south.
Photo by Victoria Lefcourt.
(left, from top to bottom)
Site plan.
Upper level plan.
Lower level plan.
Section.

(前頁)南側の上層階にとられた開口部から採光されるアトリウム。
(左、上から下に)
配置図。
上層階平面図。
低層階平面図。
断面図。

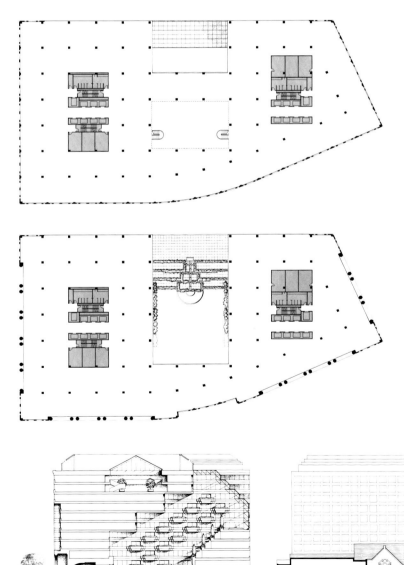

Jefferson Court

Washington, DC

ジェファーソン・コート
ワシントンDC

1984

The roots of Jefferson Court belie the popular image of Washington's Georgetown district as an area of fashionable residences, trend-setting restaurants, and exclusive retail establishments and harkens back to an earlier time when this area thrived as a port and industrial center. It is this character that is perpetuated in the design of this office and retail complex fronting on the entry axis to a large mixed-use development at the nearby waterfront.

Reminiscent of turn-of-the-century factories and warehouses, the complex is depicted as a composition of a variety of forms indicative of that industrial era. To minimize the apparent bulk of the building, the sixth floor offices lie hidden behind a sloping-glass wall that resembles a mansard roof while the uppermost floor is set back, almost concealing it totally from the street below. The red-brick structure contains such embellishments as pre-cast concrete pediments at the entries and brick ornamentation at triumvirate window groupings and the wide archways of the arcades at the retail facade and the interior courtyards.

ジェファーソン・コートのルーツを溯ると、ワシントンのジョージタウン地区の主要なイメージ——現代的な住居群、新流行のレストラン、高級店舗が立ち並ぶといった——がまちがった観念を与えていて、港町あるいは産業の中心地区として栄えた初期の姿が本来の姿であるということが理解できる。ウォーターフロント付近の大規模かつ多目的な開発地域への導入部分に面する、このオフィスと店舗の複合施設のデザインの永続性こそがここでの主題である。

世紀の変わり目を経てきた工場や倉庫群を思い起こさせるように、この複合施設は、工業時代を彷彿とさせる様々な形態の合成体として表現されている。6階のオフィスは駒形屋根に似た傾斜したガラスの壁面で覆われ、最上階はセットバックして、下の通りからはその姿がほとんど見えず、建物のヴォリュームがあからさまに見えないようにしている。赤煉瓦造の建物には、エントランス部分のプレキャスト・コンクリート製の切妻、三つで一組となった窓の煉瓦製の飾り、店舗のファサードと中庭にあるアーチ門などの装飾が付されている。

（河野裕訳）

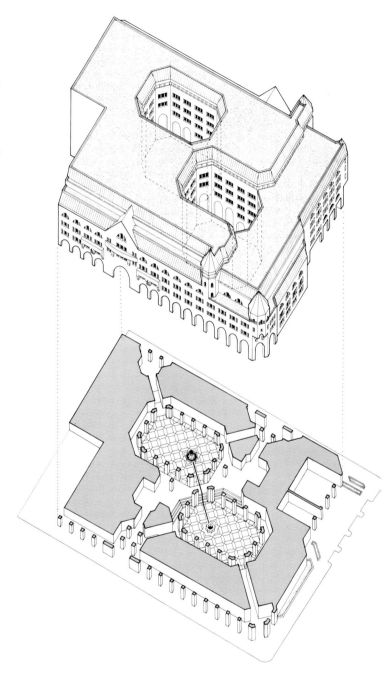

(top right) Axonometric drawing.
(bottom right) West elevation.
(opposite) View of the facade consisting of the elements such as pediment, arch, triumvirate window and arcade.
Photos (p.123 and p.125) by Carol M. Highsmith.

（右上）アクソノメトリック図。
（右下）西側立面図。
（次頁）ペディメント、アーチ、三つ組窓、アーケードなどの要素で構成された煉瓦のファサード。

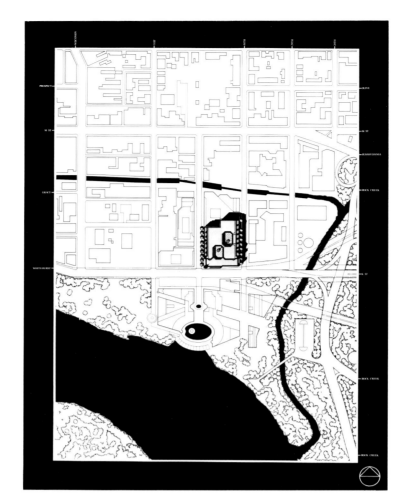

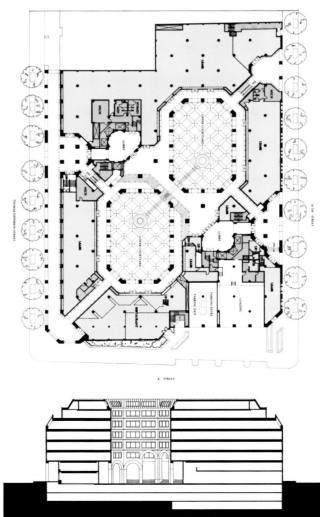

124

The Grand Hotel

Washington, DC

グランド・ホテル
ワシントンDC

1984

The 265-room Grand Hotel reflects the traditional architectural elements of the District while capturing the spirit of an intimate but elegant European hotel. Located in a redeveloping area of the city between Georgetown and the commercial core, the building and its eight-story facade appear to climb toward a corner opened by successive setbacks culminating at the dome above the main entrance. The illusion is reinforced by the placement of awnings and flags to follow the precast base as it steps from two stories at the street edge to four stories at the inverted entrance facade. Paired columns supporting the dome at the upper porch accentuate the apparent height.

The hotel is wrapped around an interior courtyard, satisfying the open space requirements while allowing the building to encompass the maximum building envelope. The interior courtyard, formally landscaped to include a terraced fountain, provides a gracious focus for a promenade restaurant following the length of the interior garden, a formal restaurant at one end and a smaller private dining room at the opposite end of the court, and the guest rooms on the floors above.

265客室のグランド・ホテルは、親しみのある雰囲気をもちつつエレガントなヨーロッパのホテルの趣きを取り入れながら、ワシントンDCの伝統的な建築エレメントを用いている。ジョージタウンと商業地域の核となる地区との間にあるこの街の再開発地域に位置するこの建物の8層分のファサードは、メイン・エントランスの上部のドームまで到達するセットバックの構成をとり、開かれた角地に向かって上昇感を出している。通り沿いの2層部分からエントランス側の4層の部分へステップするごとく日除けや旗が配置され、プレキャスト製の基壇までつながっており、幻想的な雰囲気を強めている。

ホテルは、中庭を包み込んでいて、必要とされるオープン・スペースを満足するとともに外壁面を最大限に確保できる。中庭にはテラス状の噴水があって整然とランドスケープされ、そこに面するプロムナード・レストランから優雅な景色を眺められる。

フォーマルなレストランは中庭の一方の端にあり、プライヴェート用の小さなダイニング・ルームはもう一方の端にあり、客室は次の階からはじまる。

(河野裕訳)

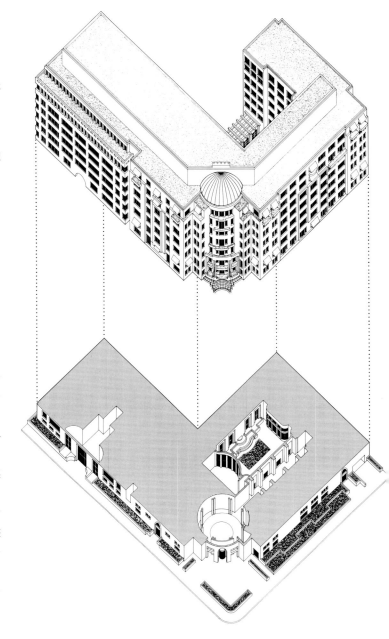

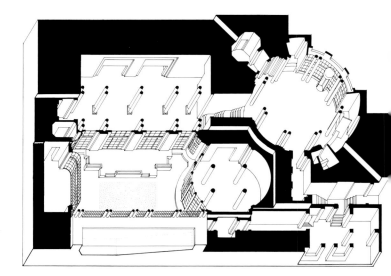

(top right) Axonometric drawing.
(bottom right) Axonometric drawing : spatial sequence.
(opposite) View of the main entrance on the northwest.
Photos (p.127 and p.129, bottom) by Maxwell MacKenzie.

(右上)アクソノメトリック図。
(右下)アクソノメトリック図：パブリックな空間のつながり。
(次頁)主玄関を北西から見る。

(right, from top to bottom)
Site plan.
Typical floor plan.
Ground floor plan.
Section.
(opposite, top) View of the courtyard.
Photo by Victoria Lefcourt.
(opposite, bottom) View of the lobby.

（右、上から下に）
配置図。
基準階平面図。
1階平面図。
断面図。
（次頁、上）中庭を見る。
（次頁、下）1階ロビーを見る。

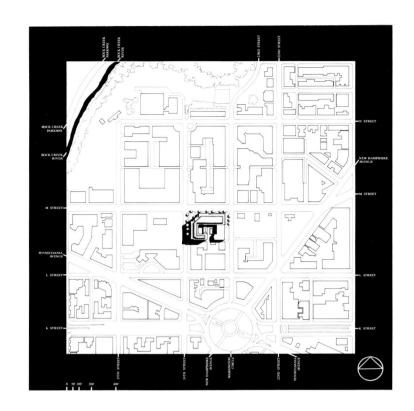

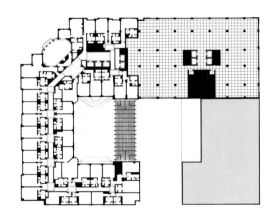

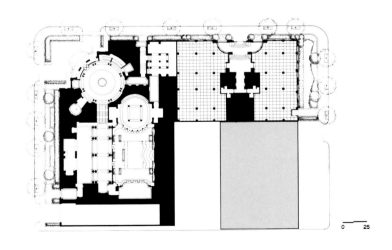

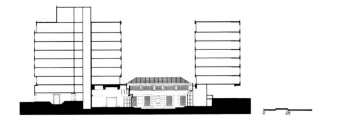

Washington Mall

Washington, DC

ワシントン・モール
ワシントンDC

1976

This Master Plan renews one of the United States' most preeminent open spaces: the Great Mall of Washington D C. The plan responds to the original vision of a Beaux Arts composition for the city's center by highlighting the surrounding historical buildings—the White House, the United States Capitol, the Washington Monument, and the Lincoln and Jefferson Memorials—in a comprehensive landscape structure. Responding to the need to better serve the growing number of visitors to the Mall, the plan orients the area to pedestrians and away from automobile traffic. Pedestrian walkways replace two vehicular streets that formerly flanked the central greensward. Light standards and benches reiterate traditional elements.

このマスター・プランは、合衆国の最も優れたオープン・スペースのひとつである「ワシントンDCの偉大なモール」を復興するものである。街のこの中心部は、広範囲にわたるランドスケープの中にあって歴史的な建造物——ホワイト・ハウス、国会議事堂、ワシントン記念碑、リンカーンとジェファーソン両大統領の記念碑——に囲まれ、強調されているが、ワシントン・モールのこの計画は、この中心部のボザールの構成という初期の構想を反映するものである。モールを訪れる人々の増加に対応できるように、歩行者のための空間を適宜定め、かつ車道から切り離した計画としている。歩行者通路は、元来、中央の緑地帯を両側から堅苦しくはさみ込んでいた2本の車道にとって代わる。街灯とベンチは歴史的な要素を反復した表現としている。

(河野裕訳)

(right) Site plan : Washington Mall/Constitution Garden.
(opposite) Night view. US Capitol is visible.
(pp.132-133) View towards the west. Washington Memorial in the middle, National Gallery of Art on the right, and Air and Space Museum on the left are visible.
Photos (pp.131-133) by Wolfgang Hoyt.
(p.132, top) Axonometric diagram.
(p.133, top) Conceptual site plan: Washington Mall/Constitution Garden.
(pp.132-133, bottom) Site section: Washington Mall/Constitution Garden.

(右)ワシントン・モールとコンスティテューション・ガーデン配置図。
(次頁)夜景。国会議事堂が見える。
(p. 132-133)西に向かって見る。中央にワシントン記念塔、右手にナショナル・ギャラリィ東館、左手に航空・宇宙博物館が見える。
(p. 132、上)アクソノメトリック・ダイアグラム。
(p. 133、上)ワシントン・モールとコンスティテューション・ガーデンとの概念配置図。
(p. 132-133、下)ワシントン・モールとコンスティテューション・ガーデンの全体断面図。

Active Projects

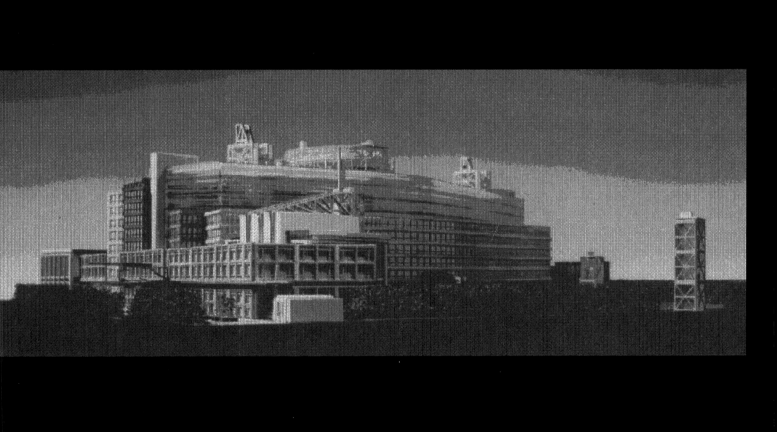

Naval Systems Command Center

Arlington, Virginia

アメリカ海軍システム・コマンド・センター
ヴァージニア州アーリントン

1992

The building program for the United States Naval Systems Command Center consists of 1,000,000 occupiable square feet of space plus a parking facility containing 1,800 spaces. The building addresses the need for a flexible facility capable of responding to the changing requirements over the structure's anticipated 100-year life span. Flexibility for the future expansion and contraction of various departments is accommodated by a large footprint with extensive areas of uninterrupted space to allow horizontal and vertical growth. Mechanical and communications flexibility is provided by multiple vertical risers (core areas) and an increased floor-to-floor height to accommodate horizontal distribution.

The site plan expresses a strong emphasis on security control while contributing to the local neighborhood by providing open space in a 1.8-acre park, various on-site amenities, and an understated design to ameliorate the impact on the community.

アメリカ海軍システム・コマンド・センターの建物には、9万3,000m²に及ぶ広さのスペースと、1,800台収容の駐車場施設が含まれている。建物には構造的な寿命としての100余年の歳月を通して要求内容が変わっても対応可能な柔軟な機構が必要である。種々の部門の将来の拡張あるいは縮小が柔軟に行なえるように、垂直・水平の両方向に自在に伸びられるような連結空間をもつ大きなエリアを確保している。多種のヴァーティカル・ライザー（コア部分）と階高を余分にとって設けられた水平方向の配送システムによって、メカニカルにも、情報伝達の面でも円滑性が保たれる。

配置計画は、セキュリティ・コントロールの心臓部を強く表現していると同時に、7,300m²の公園の中のオープン・スペースを近隣に公開し、そこでの多彩なアメニティ、そして地域の印象を改善する控え目なデザインとを付与している。

（河野裕訳）

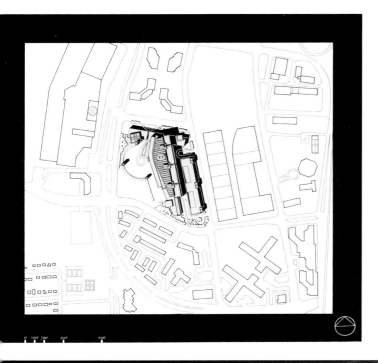

(opposite) General view from the northwest.
(below) Bird's eye view.
Photos (pp.136-137) by Jock Pottle/Esto.
(left) Site plan.
(p.138, from top to bottom) Interior of atrium.
Section.
East elevation.
(p.139, top) Tower of the conference rooms.
(p.139, bottom left) 5th thru 7th floor plan.
(p.139, bottom right) Ground floor plan.
Renderings (pp.138-139) by Richard Rochon.

（前頁）北西から見た全景。
（下）北西から俯瞰する。
（左）配置図。
（p. 138、上から下に）
アトリウム内部。
断面図。
東側立面図。
（p. 139、上）会議室のあるタワーを見る。
（p. 139、左下）5-7階平面図。
（p. 139、右下）1階平面図。

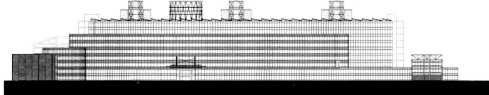

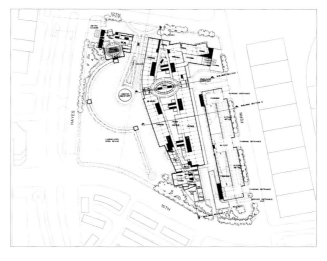

Birmann 21

São Paulo, Brazil

バーマン 21
ブラジル、サンパウロ

1994

Birmann 21 is a 375,000-square-foot investment office building that will rise in São Paulo's newest commercial sector along the Marginale. Designed as a regional headquarters address for internationally based tenants, the building will contain an employee cafeteria, a health club, and have structured parking for 900 cars. The 24-story tower is identified by the unique architectural image created by the bold vertical expression of the multi-faceted shaft culminating in its towering spire. The spire not only marks the building's place on the city's skyline but also reflects the forward-looking vision of Brazil. The building also reflects local materials and responds to climatic conditions of the southern hemisphere. The southern facade of the building, oriented to enhance views of the Pinheiros River, will be distinguished by a concave wall of glass while the northern facade and main entrance to the building will be clad in local Brazilian granites and marble and have smaller, deep set, punched windows to reduce cooling loads.

バーマン21は3万5,000㎡の巨大なオフィス・ビルで、マルジナールに沿ったサンパウロの最も新しい商業地区にそびえ立つ予定である。この建物は国際的な基盤をもつ施主の地方本部として設計され、その中には、従業員のカフェテリアやヘルス・クラブ、また、900台分の立体駐車場も計画されている。24階建てのタワーは、尖塔を頂点とし、いくつもの面によって構成された、大胆な垂直表現によってユニークな建物として識別される。その尖塔は、都市のスカイラインにおいて建物の場所を指し示すだけではなく、ブラジルの輝かしい前途を表現している。建物はその地方固有の材料を用い、また、南半球の風土に呼応してつくられている。建物の南面は、ピニェイロス川の眺望を確保し、凹状に湾曲したガラス・カーテンウォールで構成されている。一方北面および正面玄関はブラジル特有の花崗岩と大理石により構成され、冷房負荷を低減するために、窓は小さく彫りの深いものとしている。　　　　　（高木義雄訳）

(above left) View from the southwest.
(above right) View from the northwest.
Photos(above) by Roy Wright.

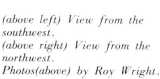

（左上）南西から見る。
（右上）北西から見る。

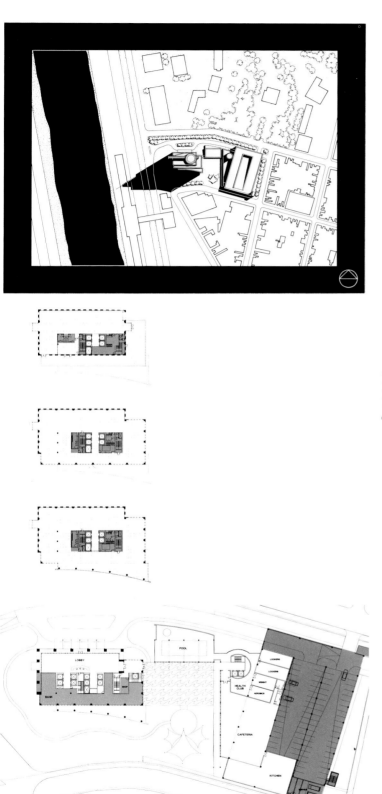

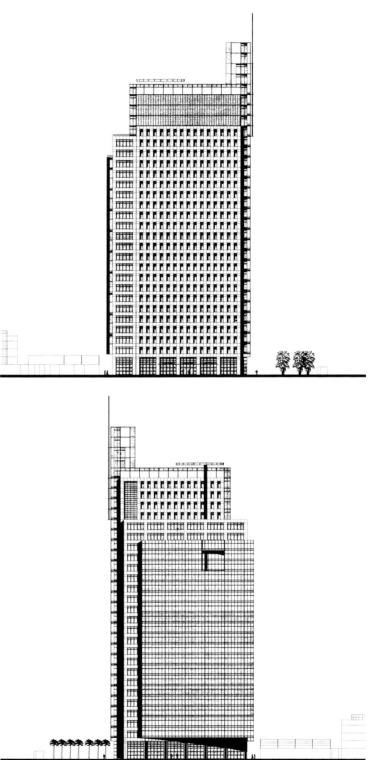

(left, from top to bottom)
Site plan.
23rd floor (executive club) plan.
21st-22nd floor plan.
12th-20th floor plan.
Ground floor plan.
(top right) North elevation.
(above right) South elevation.

（左、上から下に）
配置図。
23階役員クラブ平面図。
21-22階平面図。
12-20階平面図。
1階平面図。
（右上）北側立面図。
（右下）南側立面図。

Canary Wharf (Eastern Segment)

London, England

キャナリィ・ワーフ東側街区

英国、ロンドン

1992

The Eastern Segment of Canary Wharf is planned as an intentional contrast and complement to the initial development phases of this new and dramatic commercial center. To the west, tall towers and large buildings rise, clad primarily in stone and glass. To the east, the buildings are planned as a series of smaller structures, clad in a combination of metal, stone, and glass. The river promenade, a key public element in the project, links all the parcels together and creates a backdrop for the individual buildings, each unique in its design and contribution to the image of the project as a whole.

キャナリィ・ワーフの東側街区は、この新しく印象的な商業地域の初期の開発にたいしあえて対比的なものとなるよう計画された。初期の段階に計画された西側街区は、石とガラスとで構成された背の高いタワーがそびえている。それにたいし東側街区は、金属と石とガラスとのコンビネーションで構成された一連の低層の建物が計画された。

公共的な空間の核となる運河沿いの遊歩道はすべての街区をつなぎ、それぞれに個性的な建物の背景となる。そしてこの計画の全体としてのイメージの形成に貢献している。

(高木義雄訳)

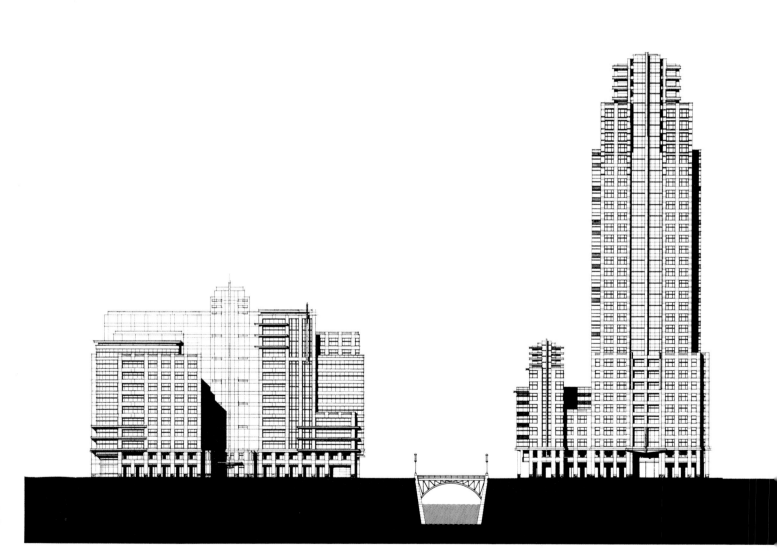

(above) South elevation:DS-3 building and BP-1 building.

(上)DS-3ビル/BP-1ビル南側立面図。

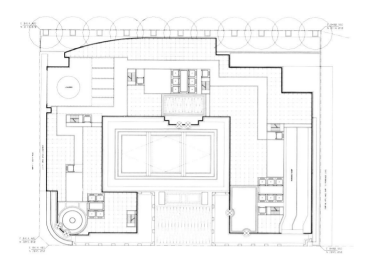

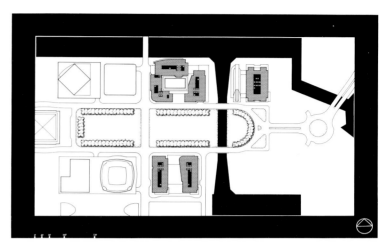

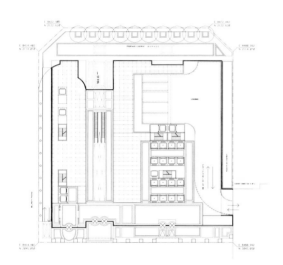

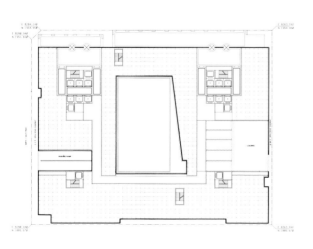

(top left) DS-3 ground floor plan.
(middle left) BP-1 ground floor plan.
(above left) DS-4 ground floor plan.
(top right) Site plan.
(above right) View of BP-1 building from the south. Rendering by Richard Rochon.

（左上）DS-3ビル1階平面図。
（左中）BP-1ビル1階平面図。
（左下）DS-4ビル1階平面図。
（右上）配置図。
（右下）BP-1ビルを南側から見る。

The Walsh Library, Seton Hall University

South Orange, New Jersey

シートン・ホール大学ウォルシュ図書館
ニュージャージィ州サウスオレンジ

1992

The Walsh Library serves as a new focal point for Seton Hall University, reaching out in a spoke-like manner to a variety of campus areas. The rotunda at the southeast corner of the structure serves as the focus of this new building. The open air circular space is placed to provide access from a number of directions while serving as the terminus for two pedestrian arcades intersecting the rotunda at two distinct levels, reflecting and responding to the site topography. The circular stair serves as the transition between the two levels, orienting users towards the library's second floor entry. The dome of the rotunda is finished in copper, a material also used to highlight the caps of the building. The exterior of the structure is clad in a soft beige pre-cast concrete with a granite inset base, reflecting the nature of materials used in other campus buildings.

シートン・ホール大学の新しい中心点の役割を果たすウォルシュ図書館は、多様なキャンパス・エリアにたいして「輪止め」のような存在となっている。建物の南東の角にあるロトンダは、この新しい建物の中心として機能する。外部に面した環状のスペースは、東西南北のどこからでもアクセスでき、また、二つの異なったレヴェルでそれぞれロトンダと交差するペデストリアン・アーケードの終着点として機能するように配置されている。二つのレヴェルを結ぶ階段は、環状に伸びて利用者を図書館の2階の入口へと誘導する。

ロトンダのドームは銅で仕上げられており、建物の頂部も同様に仕上げ、存在を際立たせている。キャンパスの他の建物で使われている材料の肌合いを考えて、外観は、花崗岩の基壇をもった、柔かなベージュ色のプレキャスト・コンクリートで覆われている。 (河野裕訳)

(above left) General view from the southeast.
(above right) View of the rotunda as main entrance.
Photos (p.144) by Eduard Hueber.
(opposite, left from top to bottom)
Upper floor plan.
Second floor plan.
(opposite, right from top to bottom)
Site plan.
East elevation.
North elevation.
(bottom) Elevation study models.
Photo by Jock Pottle/Esto.

（左上）南東から見た全景。
（右上）メイン・エントランスとなるロトンダ。
（次頁、左、上から下に）
上階平面図。
2階平面図。
（次頁、右、上から下に）
配置図。
東側立面図。
北側立面図。
（下）立面のスタディ。

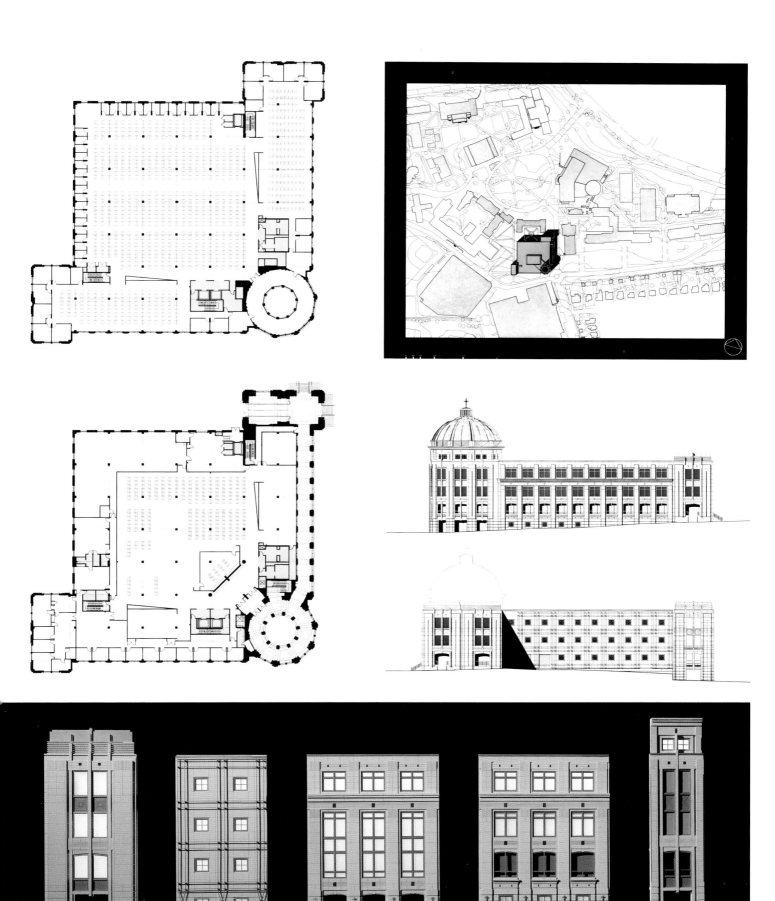

The Deerfield Academy Natatorium

Deerfield, Massachusetts

ディアフィールド・アカデミィ屋内水泳場
マサチューセッツ州ディアフィールド

1991

The Deerfield Academy Natatorium is a 37,000-square-foot addition to the existing gymnasium complex at this private secondary school located in a semi-rural area of New England. The new structure emulates and reflects the specific architectural vocabulary established by the existing campus buildings, designed by Charles Platt. The natatorium serves to architecturally link the green tabletop of the main campus to the lush playing fields below. Due to severe space limitations, it was necessary, for the first time, to extend over the edge of the "Deerfield plateau," the most extraordinary change to the Deerfield campus since the initial buildings were constructed.

Clear spanning wood trusses provide a column-free interior space and a material that responds favorably to the humidity and chemical content of the aquatic environment. Windows have been placed to eliminate glare for both the participants and the viewing gallery. Overhead lights within the truss area provide an even level of illumination over the pool area. The overhead exposed duct accommodates the return air requirements while supply air is provided at the perimeter walls at either side of each truss support.

ディアフィールド・アカデミィ屋内水泳場は、ニューイングランドの半ば田園風の地区にある中学校の既存のトレーニング施設に3,400㎡の面積を新たに加える。

新しい構造体は、チャールズ・プラットによってデザインされた既存の建物が確立した独特な建築ヴォキャブラリィを反映しつつも、劣らないものとなっている。水泳場は、建築的にキャンパスの主要な丘陵部と下に広がる草地のグラウンドとを結びつける。余地が厳しく限定されていることから、「ディアフィールド高原」の端まで拡張することが、まず第一条件であり、最初の建物群が建設されて以来のディアフィールドにおける最大の変化となった。

きれいに架け渡された木製のトラスは、水につきまとう湿気などの化学的性質にたいして好ましい材料であるとともに、無柱の空間を実現している。窓は競技関係者や観客に反射光がかからないように位置している。トラスの間の天井照明は、プールの上に均一な照度がとれるように設けられている。上部に剝き出しになった排気ダクトはリターン・エアの容量を調整し、給気は、両側のトラスの支持部分の両脇に立つ給気ダクトより行なわれる。 (河野裕訳)

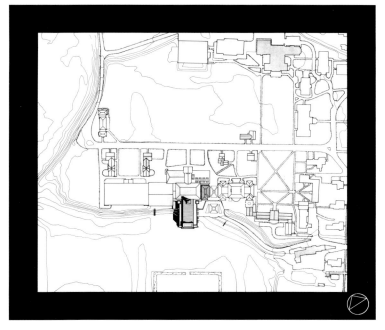
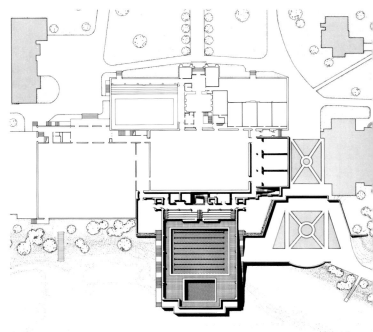

(above left) Site plan.
(above right) Upper level plan.
(opposite)View from the south.
Rendering by Richard Rochon.

(左上)配置図。
(右上)上階平面図。
(次頁)南側のグラウンドから見る。

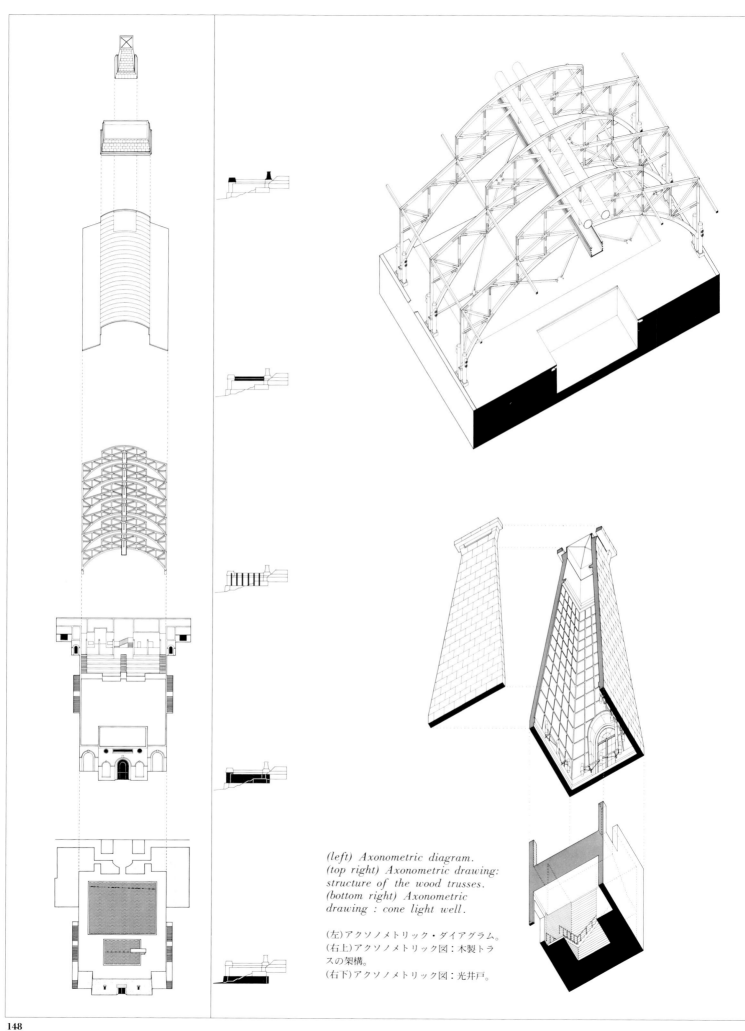

(left) Axonometric diagram.
(top right) Axonometric drawing:
structure of the wood trusses.
(bottom right) Axonometric
drawing : cone light well.

(左)アクソノメトリック・ダイアグラム。
(右上)アクソノメトリック図：木製トラ
スの架構。
(右下)アクソノメトリック図：光井戸。

(top left) Model showing the structure of wood trusses and the exposed ducts for air conditioning.
Photo by Jock Pottle/Esto.
(bottom left) Section.

(左上)木製トラスの架構と露出された空調ダクトを示す模型写真。
(左下)断面図。

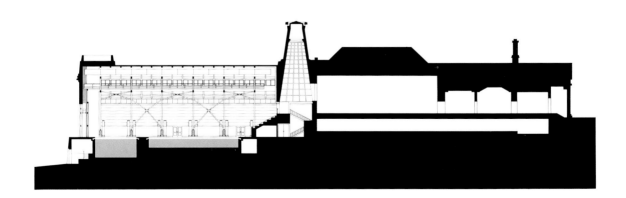

University of Cincinnati

Cincinnati, Ohio

シンシナティ大学
オハイオ州シンシナティ

1992

The Auxiliary Swing Space Building at the University of Cincinnati is situated on a prominent site at the Southeast entry to the campus. It functions as the gateway building from the downtown area of the city, leading to a proposed Performing Arts Center.
The building, consisting of three parts, will respond to the university's newly-adopted master plan, a collision of old and new grids. A two-story base, rectilinear to the street, responds to the recently established plan, and a high-rise tower is rotated to reflect the original campus grid. Finally, a parking garage concealing over 600 cars is delineated as an architectural expression to form a backdrop to the other building components.

シンシナティ大学のオーグジリアリィ・スウィング・スペースはキャンパスの南東入口に面し、非常によく見えるところである。それは、ダウンタウンからの玄関として機能し、提案されている舞台芸術センターへと導く。三つの部分からなる建物は新旧グリッドの不調和を考慮しながら新しいマスター・プランに適応していくことになる。2層分の基壇部分は道に沿って直線をなし、新しく設定されたプランに適応する一方、高層のタワーは、元来のキャンパスのグリッドに合わせて首を振る。
また、600台以上の車を収容する駐車場は建築的には他の建物要素にたいする背景を形成するよう表現されている。 （高木義雄訳）

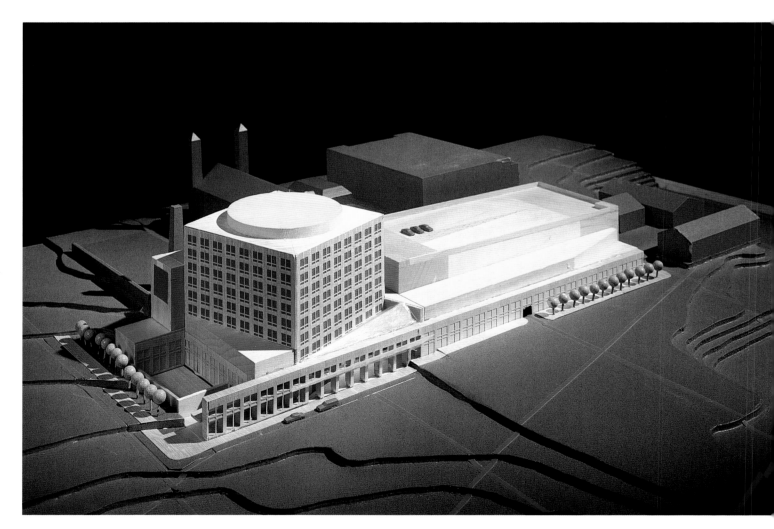

(above) General view from the north.
Photo by Bryan Nolan.
(opposite, left from top to bottom)
Site plan.
Upper level plan.
Computer drawing : north elevation.

(opposite, right from top to bottom)
Campus plan.
Ground floor plan.

（上）北側から見た全景。
（次頁、左上から左下に）
配置図。
上階平面図。
コンピュータ・ドローイング：北側立面図。

（次頁、右上から右下に）
キャンパス・プラン。
1階平面図。

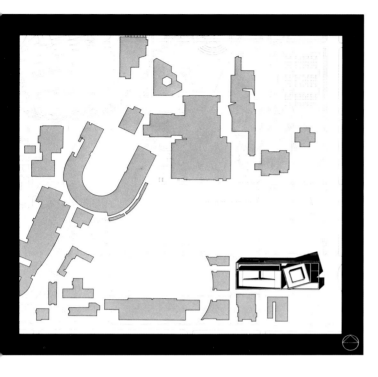

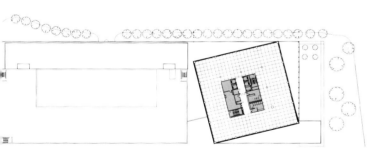

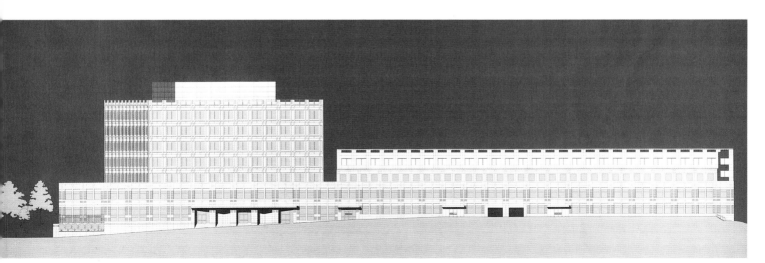

Dulles International Airport

Washington, DC

ダレス国際空港
ワシントンDC

1997

Dulles International Airport is being expanded to accommodate more than twice the number of passengers currently being served. The elegant Main Terminal, a landmark originally designed by Eero Saarinen, is to be extended and reconfigured to meet the projected growth. The terminal's catenary roof structure and podium are being doubled in length to house in two levels the curbside, ticketing, check-in, baggage claim, and support functions. Expansion space needed for baggage handling, security, and passenger transport to airside is provided in two additional levels beneath the apron. Six new Midfield Concourse buildings, each containing 24 gates, are linked to the Main Terminal by a new, two-mile people-mover system. The recently constructed International Arrivals Building sets a new standard for customs and immigration facilities in the United States.

ダレス国際空港は現在の2倍の収容能力を確保するために、拡張工事中である。エーロ・サーリネンによって設計された優雅なメイン・ターミナルは、横に延長され、技術的な部分の改装が行なわれる。もちろん、歴史的な建築物にたいして与える視覚的影響は最小限になるように配慮している。

地上レヴェルのカテナリィ曲線の屋根とそれを支える列柱はそのままの姿で拡張され、2層にわたって歩道、チケッティング、チェックイン、バゲージ・クレイムなどの機能が収容される。その他貨物操作場、セキュリティおよび旅客の搭乗口までの移動通路はエプロンの下、2層にわたって配置される。

それぞれに24のゲートをもった六つのコンコース・ビルディングは、3.2kmにわたる旅客移動システムが新設されメイン・ターミナルとつながれる。また新たに建設された国際便の到着ターミナル・ビルディングは、合衆国における税関・入国管理施設の新しい基準を示すものである。　　　　（高木義雄訳）

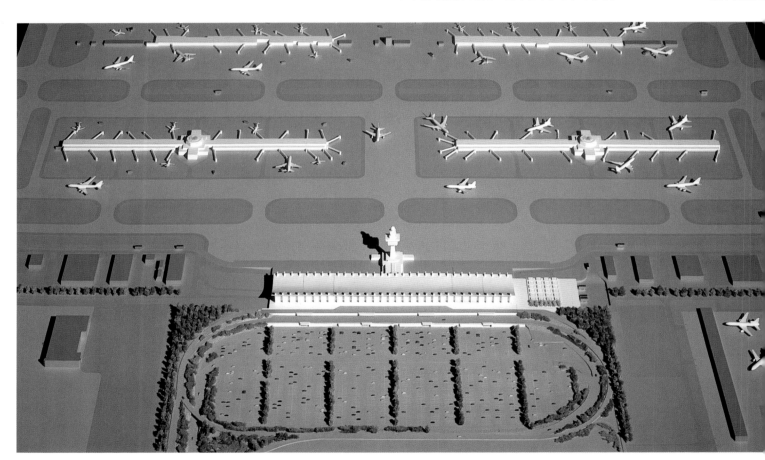

(above) View of the main terminal building in the front and concourse buildings at the back.
Photo by Wolfgang Hoyt.
(right) Axonometric drawing: main terminal expansion.
(opposite) Computer drawing: view of the terminal building from the northwest.
(opposite, top) Site plan.
(opposite, bottom) Baggage handling.
Photo by Robert Lautman.

（上）手前にメイン・ターミナル、後方にコンコース・ビルディングを見る。
（右）メイン・ターミナルの増築。
（次頁）北西よりターミナル・ビルを見る。
（次頁、上）配置図。
（次頁、下）手荷物受取室を見る。

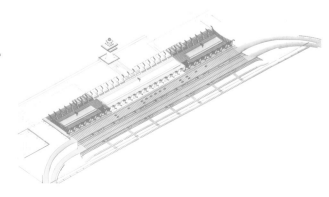

Yerba Buena Office Towers

San Francisco, California
in collaboration with Frank O. Gehry & Associates
イェルバ・ブエナ・オフィス・タワー
カリフォルニア州サンフランシスコ
（フランク・ゲーリィとの共同設計）
1989

This project consists of two separate office towers located on Third Street between Howard and Mission Streets, within a 24-acre Yerba Buena Gardens urban renewal project. The two office towers stand on opposite corners of the block and flank the proposed Museum of Modern Art. The North Tower, designed by Frank Gehry, will contain 500,000 square feet in 29 stories; the South Tower will contain 350,000 square feet in 23 stories. Designed to act as bookends for the museum, the towers work together with the adjoining Pacific Telephone Building to engage in a spiraling dialogue.

この計画はサード・ストリート沿いに並ぶ、2本の異なるオフィス・タワーからなる。ハワード・ストリートとミッション・ストリートとにはさまれた、広さ9.7haのイェルバ・ブエナ公園の再開発街区にこの計画は位置する。
それぞれのオフィス・タワーは一つの街区の互いに反対の角に面し、その2本のタワーの間には近代美術館が企画されている。フランク・ゲーリィによって計画されている北側のタワーは延床面積4万6,000㎡、地上29階建て、またわれわれの計画している南側のタワーは延床面積3万3,000㎡、地上23階建てである。
2本のタワーは近代美術館のブックエンドに見えるがごとくデザインされ、隣接するパシフィック・テレフォン・ビルも合わせて3本のタワーは螺旋を描いて上昇していく。　　　　　　　　（高木義雄訳）

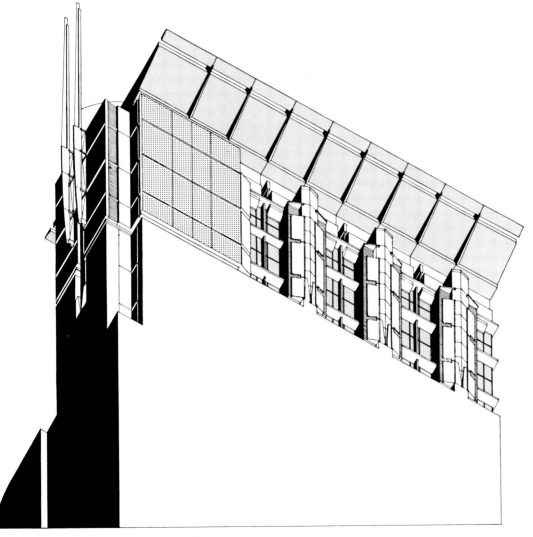

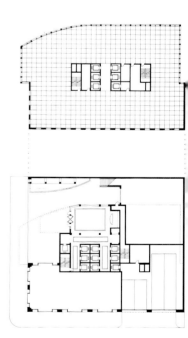

(above left) Axonometric drawing: the top of building.
(top right) Typical floor plan.
(bottom right) Ground floor plan.
(opposite, left) South elevation.
(opposite, top right) Site plan.
(opposite, bottom right) View from the southeast.
Rendering by Richard Rochon.

（左上）アクソノメトリック図：頂部を見る。
（右上）基準階平面図。
（右下）1階平面図。
（次頁、左）南側立面図。
（次頁、右上）配置図。
（次頁、右下）南東から見る。

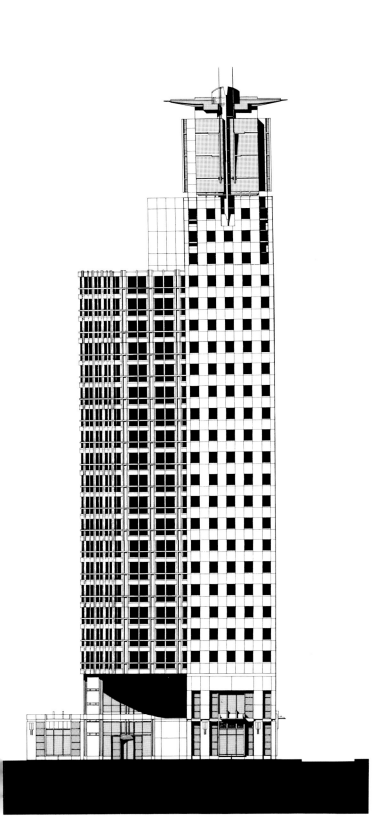

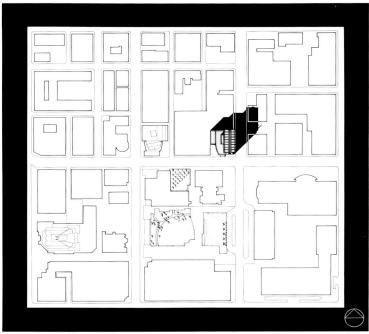

Barajas

Madrid, Spain

バラハス

スペイン、マドリッド

1989

This low-rise office complex is located east of Madrid, adjacent to the city's international airport. The 370,000-square-foot complex presents itself as three buildings between which are two distinctive courtyards, one a circular water garden and the other a square enclave of foliage. A bar of office space joins the three buildings forming the third side of the courtyards.

In elevation, the building exhibits a tripartite organization with precast at its base, Roman brick in the middle, and a precast and metal loggia at the building top. A curved curtain wall at the entry facades mediates these three elements. To maximize natural light, the building is no wider than 18 meters at any one point and 3 meters from floor to ceiling. Parking for 900 cars is provided in three levels below grade.

この低層オフィス・ビルの複合体はマドリッドの東部、国際空港に隣接している。延床面積3万4,000㎡のこの建物は三つの建物に見えるように計画され、その間に二つの特徴のある中庭をはさむ。一つは円形の水の庭園、そしてもう一つは正方形に刈り込まれた植栽の庭園である。中庭に面して三つの建物をつなぐように折線状のオフィスが、中庭の一面を構成する。

この建物は立面において3層構成を呈する。基壇にはプレキャスト・コンクリートを、中段にはローマ煉瓦を、そして頂部にはプレキャスト・コンクリートと金属でできた回廊をそれぞれ配し、正面の緩やかな円を描くカーテンウォールがその3層を調和させる。

自然光を最大限利用するためにこの建物は天井高を3m確保し、窓からの距離が18m以上にはならないように配慮している。また地下には3層にわたって900台が収容できる駐車場が設置されている。

(高木義雄訳)

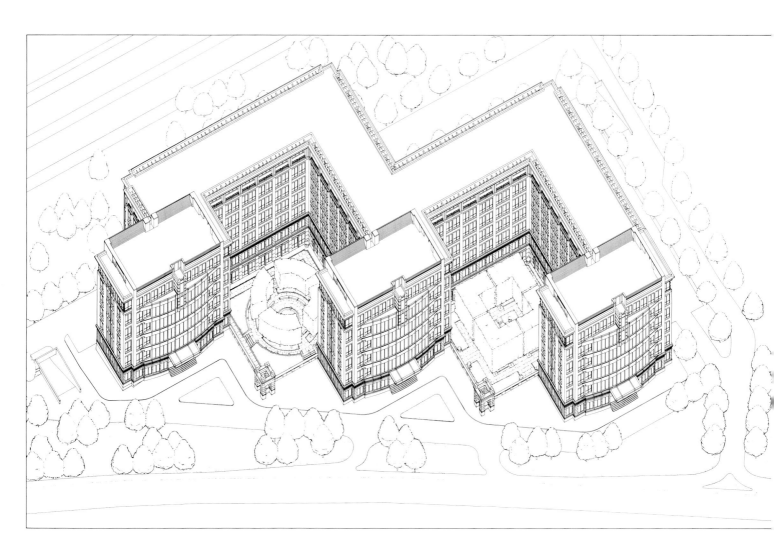

(above) Axonometric drawing: a circular water garden and a square enclave of foliage are visible.
(opposite, top) Computer drawings.
(opposite, middle) Site plan.
(opposite, bottom) Ground floor plan.

(上)アクソノメトリック図：円形の水の庭園と正方形に刈り込まれた植栽の庭園が見える。
(次頁、上)コンピュータ・ドローイング。
(次頁、中)配置図。
(次頁、下)1階平面図。

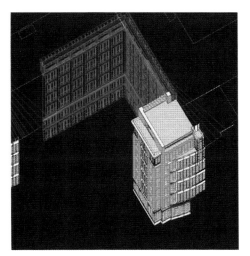

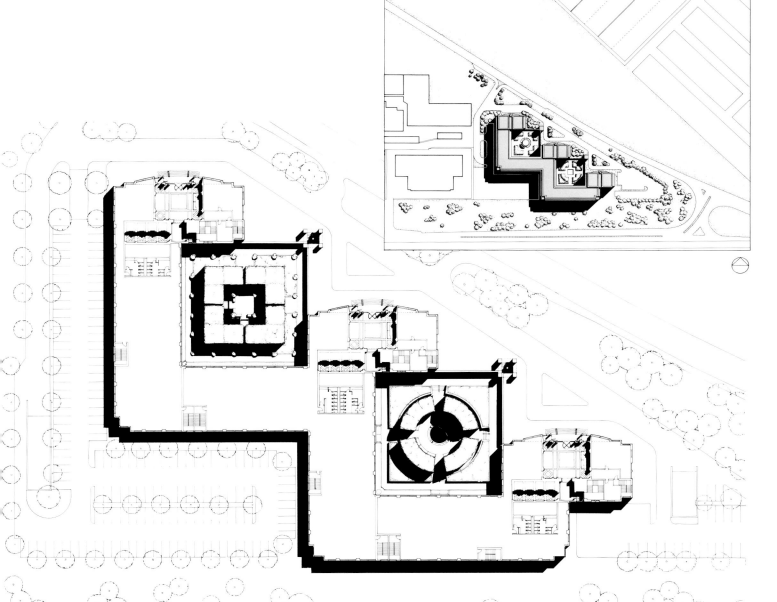

MASS MoCA

North Adams, Massachusetts
in collaboration with Frank O. Gehry & Associates; Venturi, Rauch and Scott Brown; and Bruner/Cott & Associates

マサチューセッツ現代美術館
マサチューセッツ州ノース・アダムス
（フランク・ゲーリィ、ヴェンチューリ・ローチ・アンド・スコット・ブラウン、ブルナー／コット・アンド・アソシエイツとの共同設計）
1989

This master plan converts an old mill complex, consisting of 28 historic buildings, into a cultural and commercial center containing the world's largest museum of contemporary art. The site is located three hours from New York City and Boston, Massachusetts on the Hoosic River in the Berkshire hills. The additive industrial imagery of the complex is retained as museum and visitor circulation is introduced. Existing buildings are converted to gallery space, with shops, restaurants, cafes, and inn rooms interspersed. Fabrication space, artist studios, and housing are also provided. The museum encompasses over 400,000 square feet, with 250,000 square feet of related commercial and residential development.

このマスター・プランは、28棟からなる製粉工場のコンプレックスを文化および商業施設の複合体に改装する計画である。その中には世界最大の現代美術の美術館も計画されている。この敷地はニューヨーク、ボストンから3時間の位置、マサチューセッツ州のフージック川のほとり、バークシャーの丘にある。このコンプレックスの増築を重ねてきた工場のイメージは、美術館として残され、来館者の導入部となる。既存の建物は、展示空間となり、店舗、レストラン、カフェ、宿泊室などが散在する。また、製作場、芸術家のアトリエ、住居も計画されている。美術館は3万7,000㎡以上の面積をもち、その内の2万3,000㎡は商業および住居の開発である。　　　　　　　（高木義雄訳）

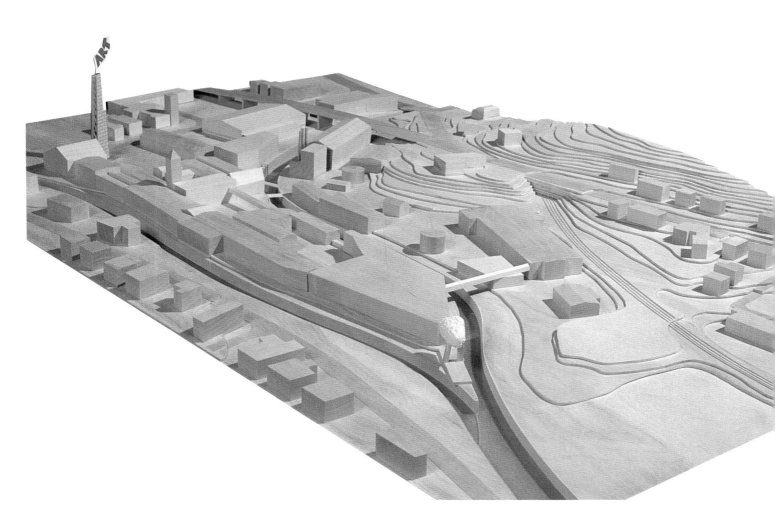

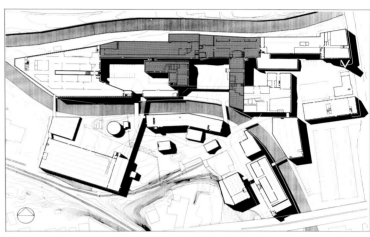

(opposite,top) View from the west.
Photo by Silas Chiow / SOM.
(opposite, bottom) South elevation and section of the art museum and the inn.

(above right) Site plan.
(above left) Existing condition. Photo by Silas Chiow / SOM.
(below) Partial elevation of the art museum and section of the inn.

（前頁、上）西側から見た全景。
（前頁、下）美術館・宿泊室南側立面図。
（右上）配置図。
（左上）現状。
（中）美術館・宿泊室南側部分立面図・断面図。

Competition Projects

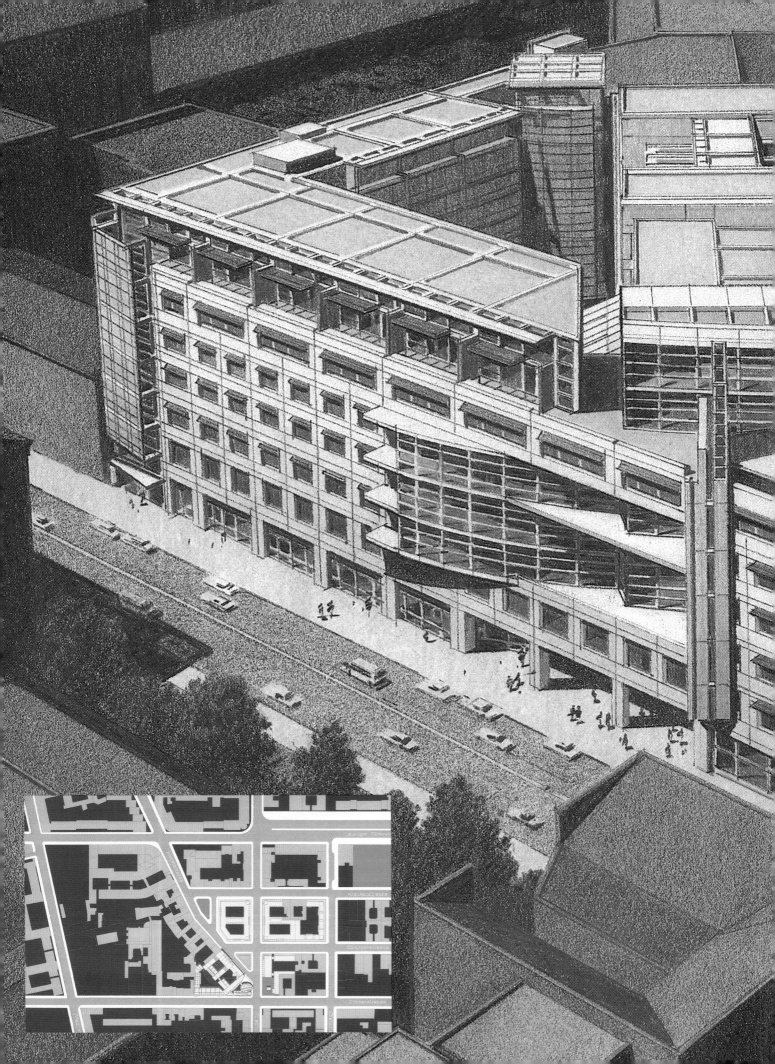

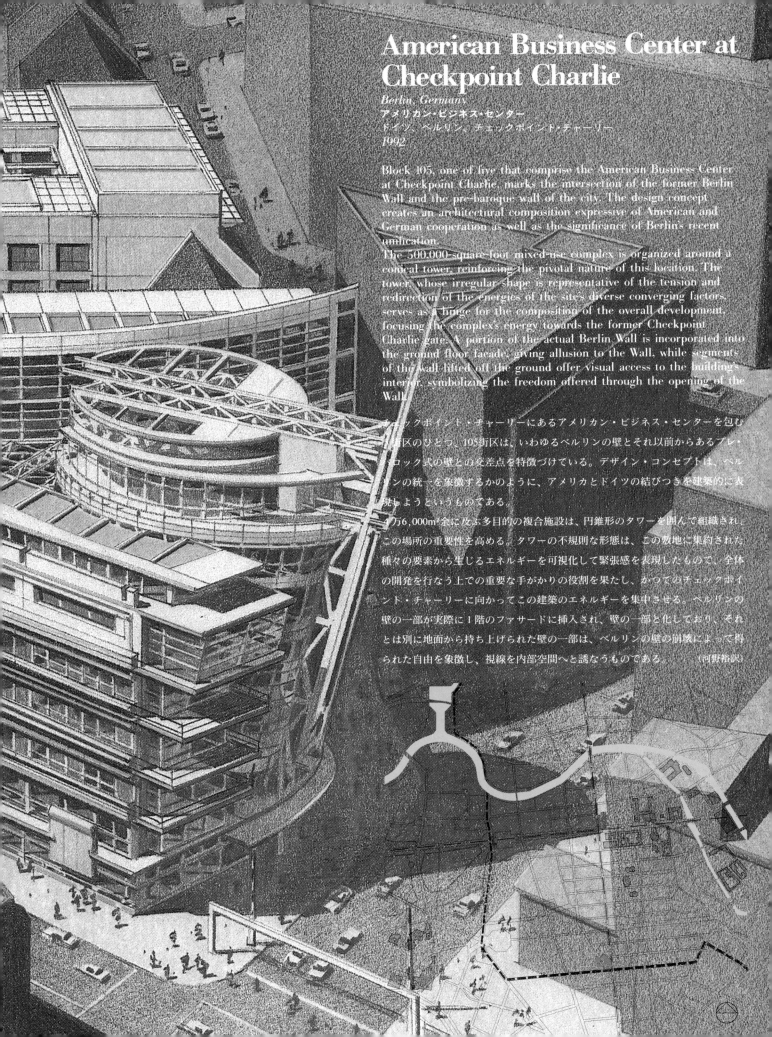

American Business Center at Checkpoint Charlie

Berlin, Germany
アメリカン・ビジネス・センター
ドイツ ベルリン。チェックポイント・チャーリー
1992

Block 105, one of five that comprise the American Business Center at Checkpoint Charlie, marks the intersection of the former Berlin Wall and the pre-baroque wall of the city. The design concept creates an architectural composition expressive of American and German cooperation as well as the significance of Berlin's recent unification.

The 500,000-square-foot mixed-use complex is organized around a conical tower, reinforcing the pivotal nature of this location. The tower, whose irregular shape is representative of the tension and redirection of the energies of the site's diverse converging factors, serves as a hinge for the composition of the overall development, focusing the complex's energy towards the former Checkpoint Charlie gate. A portion of the actual Berlin Wall is incorporated into the ground floor facade, giving allusion to the Wall, while segments of the wall lifted off the ground offer visual access to the building's interior, symbolizing the freedom offered through the opening of the Wall.

チェックポイント・チャーリーにあるアメリカン・ビジネス・センターを包む街区のひとつ、105街区は、いわゆるベルリンの壁とそれ以前からあるプレ・バロック式の壁との交差点を特徴づけている。デザイン・コンセプトは、ベルリンの統一を象徴するかのように、アメリカとドイツの結びつきを建築的に表現しようというものである。

4万6,000m²余に及ぶ多目的の複合施設は、円錐形のタワーを囲んで組織され、この場所の重要性を高める。タワーの不規則な形態は、この敷地に集約された種々の要素から生じるエネルギーを可視化して緊張感を表現したもので、全体の開発を行なう上での重要な手がかりの役割を果たし、かつてのチェックポイント・チャーリーに向かってこの建築のエネルギーを集中させる。ベルリンの壁の一部が実際に1階のファサードに挿入され、壁の一部と化しており、それとは別に地面から持ち上げられた壁の一部は、ベルリンの壁の崩壊によって得られた自由を象徴し、視線を内部空間へと誘なうものである。　　　　　(河野裕訳)

(pp.162-163) Bird's eye view from the southeast. Rendering by Richard Rochon.
(p.162, bottom) Computer drawing:site plan.
(p.163, bottom) Diagram:site plan.
(above) Computer drawing:south elevation.

(below left) 3rd-5th floor plan.
(below right) Ground floor plan.
(opposite, bottom left) View from the southeast.
(opposite, bottom right) View of the northeast corner.
Photos (p.165) by Bryan Nolan.

(p.162-163)南東側から俯瞰する。
(p.162、下)コンピュータ・ドローイング：配置図。
(p.163、下)ダイアグラム：配置図。
(上)コンピュータ・ドローイング：南側立面図。
(左下)3-5階平面図。
(右下)1階平面図。
(次頁、左下)南東から見る。
(次頁、右下)北東のコーナーを見る。

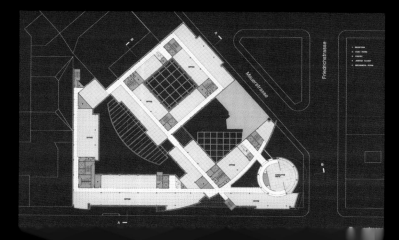

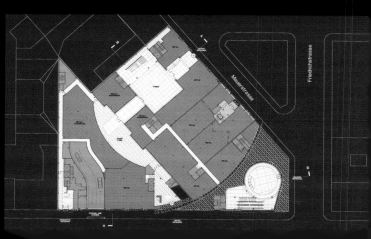

Whitehall Ferry Terminal

New York, New York

ホワイトホール・フェリィ・ターミナル
ニューヨーク州ニューヨーク

1992

The design for the Whitehall Ferry Terminal addresses the necessary functional requirements while creating a dynamic and inviting facility that anchors the southern edge of Battery Park at the southern tip of Manhattan. The focus of the terminal complex is the entrance pavilion, a monumental form serving as a new landmark that will take its place in the park in a juxtaposition to the existing monuments of Castle Clinton and the War Memorial. The pavilion organizes the variety of circulation patterns within the complex, providing direct subway access as well as providing a transition to the park, the ferry arrival/departure area, the restaurant, and the rooftop garden. The rooftop garden, accessed by ramps reminiscent of New York suspension bridges, allows the park to reach to the river's edge and the pedestrian promenade to continue through the site, establishing this new terminal complex as an integral piece of Battery Park and an important addition to the waterfront area.

ホワイトホール・フェリィ・ターミナルのデザインは、機能上の必要条件を満たしていると同時に、マンハッタンの南端、さらにバッテリィ・パークの南端に定着したダイナミックで魅力的な施設を生みだしている。ターミナルの複合施設の中心には、新しいランドマークとしての機能を果たすように記念碑的な形態をしたエントランス・パヴィリオンがある。これは、既存のクリントン城や戦争記念碑と並んで公園の中に位置づけられる。パヴィリオンは、複合施設の中の様々なサーキュレーションのパターンを内包しており、地下鉄から直接アクセスできると同時に、公園、フェリィの発着所、レストラン、屋上庭園への分岐点として機能する。

屋上庭園へは、ニューヨークのサスペンション・ブリッジを思わせる傾斜路からアクセスできる。屋上に庭園を設けることで、公園の周辺への広がりや、敷地をつらぬく遊歩道の連続性が確保される。これらによって、この新しいターミナルの複合施設は、バッテリィ・パークに欠かせない一要素として、あるいはウォーターフロント・エリアにおける重要なプロジェクトとして確立される。

（河野裕訳）

(pp.166-167) View from the
southwest.
Photo by Jock Pottle / Esto.
(opposite, bottom) Site plan.
(top right) Section.
(bottom right) Interior of the
rotunda.
Rendering by Richard Rochon.

(p.166-167)南西から見る。
(前頁、下)配置図。
(右上)断面図。
(右下)ロトンダの内部を見る。

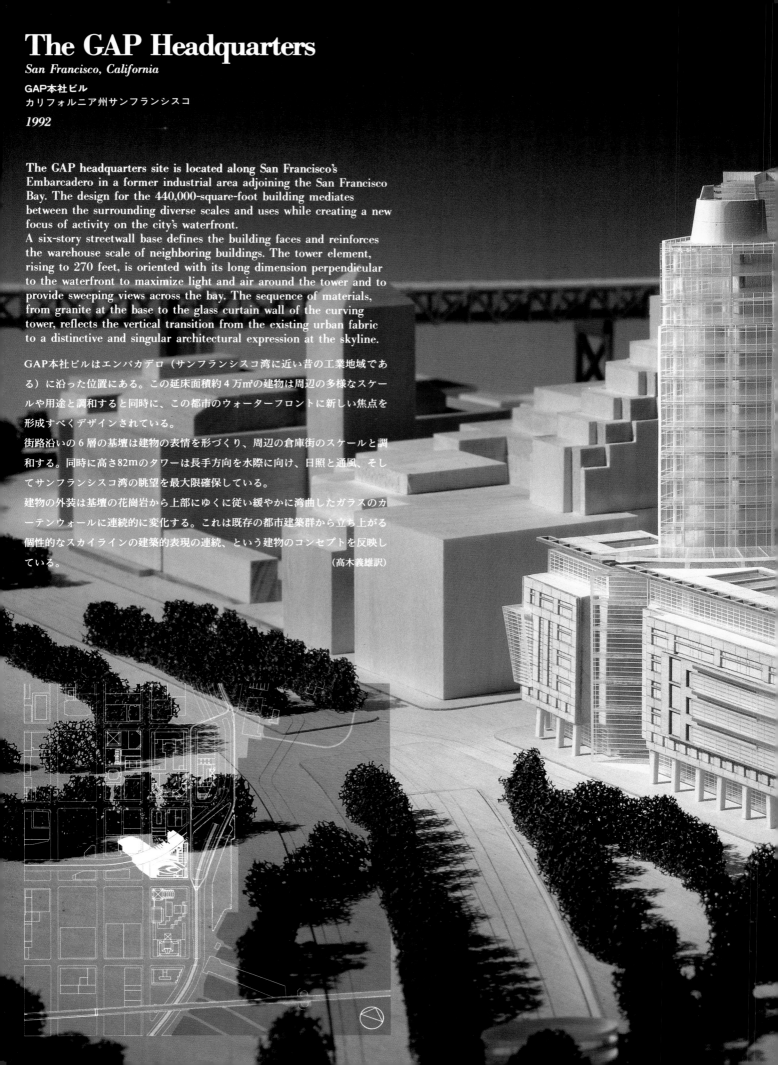

The GAP Headquarters
San Francisco, California

GAP本社ビル
カリフォルニア州サンフランシスコ

1992

The GAP headquarters site is located along San Francisco's Embarcadero in a former industrial area adjoining the San Francisco Bay. The design for the 440,000-square-foot building mediates between the surrounding diverse scales and uses while creating a new focus of activity on the city's waterfront.

A six-story streetwall base defines the building faces and reinforces the warehouse scale of neighboring buildings. The tower element, rising to 270 feet, is oriented with its long dimension perpendicular to the waterfront to maximize light and air around the tower and to provide sweeping views across the bay. The sequence of materials, from granite at the base to the glass curtain wall of the curving tower, reflects the vertical transition from the existing urban fabric to a distinctive and singular architectural expression at the skyline.

GAP本社ビルはエンバカデロ（サンフランシスコ湾に近い昔の工業地域である）に沿った位置にある。この延床面積約4万㎡の建物は周辺の多様なスケールや用途と調和すると同時に、この都市のウォーターフロントに新しい焦点を形成すべくデザインされている。

街路沿いの6層の基壇は建物の表情を形づくり、周辺の倉庫街のスケールと調和する。同時に高さ82mのタワーは長手方向を水際に向け、日照と通風、そしてサンフランシスコ湾の眺望を最大限確保している。

建物の外装は基壇の花崗岩から上部にゆくに従い緩やかに湾曲したガラスのカーテンウォールに連続的に変化する。これは既存の都市建築群から立ち上がる個性的なスカイラインの建築的表現の連続、という建物のコンセプトを反映している。

（高木義雄訳）

(pp.168-169) View from the north.
(opposite, bottom) Site plan.
(above) View from the San Francisco Bay on the northeast.
Photos (pp.168-169) by Bryan Nolan.
(below) Axonometric drawing: view from the east.

（p.168-169）北から見る。
（前頁、下）配置図。
（上）北東側のサンフランシスコ湾より見る。
（下）アクソノメトリック図：東側から見る。

Logan International Airport

Boston, Massachusetts

ローガン国際空港
マサチューセッツ州ボストン

1992

Logan Airport, located at the edge of Boston Harbor, is experiencing a dramatic increase in air traffic, requiring a modernization program to meet additional capacity requirements. This project establishes design guidelines to ensure consistency in the implementation of the modernization program and the realization of a functional, cohesive airport. The guidelines develop an overall airport image and the architectural vocabulary to be used in all development and renovation projects undertaken as part of the program. Components to which the guidelines will apply include a new landside terminal, two new airside concourses, an international arrivals building, and a people-mover system.

ボストン港の端部に位置するローガン空港では、航空交通量が劇的に増加したためにさらなる収容能力の必要性に見合った現代的なプログラムが求められている。このプロジェクトは、現代的なプログラムの履行あるいは、機能的に完結した空港の実現に際して、デザインの一貫性を保つための指針を確立するものである。空港全体のイメージや建築的な言語――プログラムのもとに着手されるすべての開発や修復計画に用いられる――が、この指針によりさらに広がりを見せる。
この指針に定められている構成要素には、新しい地上ターミナル、二つの新しいエアサイド・コンコース、国際線到着ビル、利用客の移動のためのシステム「動く歩道」が含まれている。　　　　　　　　　　　　（河野裕訳）

(pp. 170-171)Computer drawing: interior of the airside concourse.
(below) Site plan.
(opposite,top right) Computer drawing:exterior view of the structure.
(opposite,middle right) Computer drawing:sectional perspective view.
(opposite,bottom right) Perspective view from the northwest.

(p.170-171)コンピュータ・ドローイング：エアサイド・コンコース内部を見る。
（下）配置図。
（次頁、右上）コンピュータ・ドローイング：外側から見た架構。
（次頁、右中）コンピュータ・ドローイング：断面を見る。
（次頁、右下）北西から見る。

Walk
On Left
Stand
on Right

↑ Terminal B
  Air Transportation Center
  Baggage Claim
  Restrooms

↑ Elevator
↑ Telephone
↑ Gates A1-A20
→ Passenger Service
↑ Information

Gate
A 2

Gate
A2

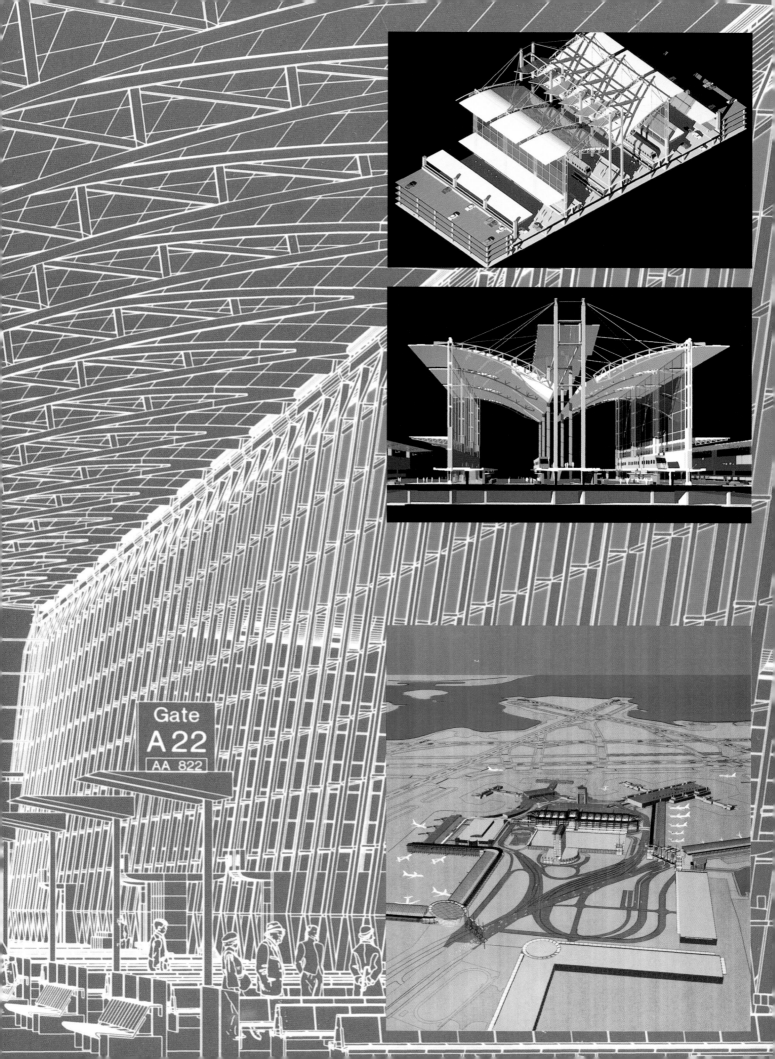

Gate
A22
AA 822

The Istanbul Culture and Art Center

Istanbul, Turkey

イスタンブール文化芸術センター
トルコ、イスタンブール
1991

The Istanbul Culture and Art Center, containing Concert and Recital Halls, an Amphitheater, and ancillary support space is designed as a modern reflection of a traditional Ottoman *kulliye*. The organization of the complex establishes an hierarchy for the varied program functions and also responds to the site's wooded hills and microclimatic conditions.

The geometric representation of the building volumes relates directly to their functions. The linear buildings, housing offices and support areas, form a backdrop for the volumetric expression of the concert and recital halls. Located at the center of the complex, the recital hall is represented as a cylindrical volume. The Concert Hall, the main focus of the Culture and Art Center, is represented as a rectangular volume topped by a vault that is reminiscent of the imperial mosques of the Istanbul skyline. A cascading glass enclosure attaches to the north of the building, serving as a transition to the adjacent linear building while creating a roof suggestive of the movement associated with the stair and reflective of the rolling hills surrounding the site.

イスタンブール文化芸術センターは、コンサート・ホール、リサイタル・ホール、円形劇場とそれらに付属する管理諸施設を含み、伝統的なオスマン・トルコ時代のキュリエ（モスクを中心とした教育施設群）を現代感に反映したデザインがなされている。コンプレックスの構成は、様々な施設プログラムにたいしてある種の階級づけをなしたものであり、また、この敷地の生い茂った森に覆われた丘と、局部的な気候条件とに対応したものである。

建物の形態の幾何学的な表現は、これらの機能を直接反映している。劇場事務所と管理諸施設の建物は、リニアに配置され、コンサート・ホールとリサイタル・ホールの圧倒的なヴォリュームの表現にたいして背景を形づくっている。リサイタル・ホールは、コンプレックスの中央部に位置し、円筒状のヴォリュームとして表現されている。文化芸術センターの主要施設であるコンサート・ホールは、イスタンブールのスカイラインに威厳をもってそびえるモスクを思わせるヴォールト屋根を載せた矩形のヴォリュームとして表現されている。ホールの北側に設置されたカスケード状の階段は、ガラスで囲まれており、隣接する細長い建物への転調の役割を果たす。さらにそこには、階段を暗示するような動きのある形態、あるいは、敷地を取り囲むうねった丘を反映するような形態をした屋根が架けられている。　　　　　　　　　　　　　　　　　　［野裕訳］

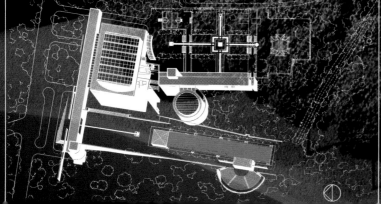

*(pp.172-173) General view
from the southwest.
Photo by Bryan Nolan.
(opposite, bottom) Site plan.
(top) West elevation.
(above) North elevation.*

（p.172-173）南西から見た全景。
（前頁、下）配置図。
（上）西側立面図。
（下）北側立面図。

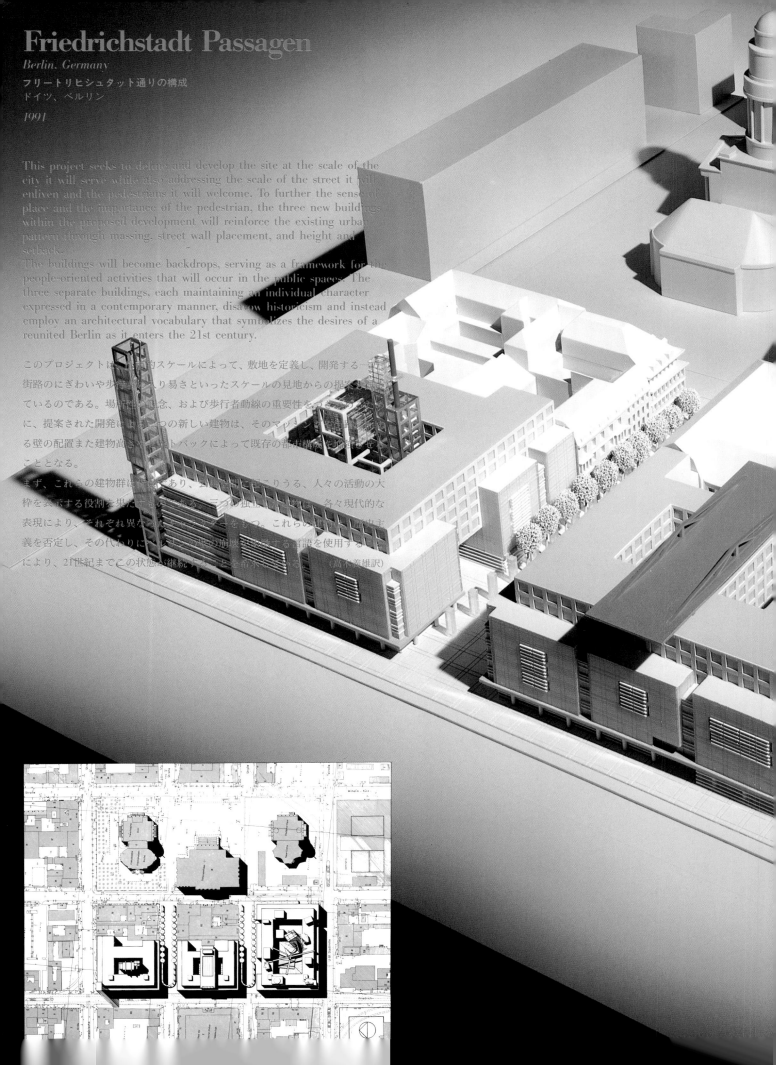

Friedrichstadt Passagen

Berlin, Germany

フリートリヒシュタット通りの構成
ドイツ、ベルリン

1991

This project seeks to define and develop the site at the scale of the city it will serve while also addressing the scale of the street it will enliven and the pedestrians it will welcome. To further the sense of place and the importance of the pedestrian, the three new buildings within the proposed development will reinforce the existing urban pattern through massing, street wall placement, and height and setback.

The buildings will become backdrops, serving as a framework for the people-oriented activities that will occur in the public spaces. The three separate buildings, each maintaining an individual character expressed in a contemporary manner, disavow historicism and instead employ an architectural vocabulary that symbolizes the desires of a reunited Berlin as it enters the 21st century.

このプロジェクトは、都市的スケールによって、敷地を定義し、開発する一方、街路のにぎわいや歩行者のより易さといったスケールの見地からの提案がなされているのである。場所性の概念、および歩行者動線の重要性をさらに推し進めるために、提案された開発による三つの新しい建物は、そのマッシングと前面道路に面する壁の配置また建物高さやセットバックによって既存の都市構成を強調させることとなる。

まず、これらの建物群は背景であり、公共空間に起こりうる、人々の活動の大枠を表示する役割を果たすものである。三つの独立した建物に、各々現代的な表現により、それぞれ異なるキャラクターをもつ。これらの建物は歴史主義を否定し、その代わりにベルリンの望の前提を象徴する言語を使用することにより、21世紀までこの状態が継続することを希求している。　　(葛木養雄訳)

(pp.174-175) General view
from the southwest.
(p.174, bottom) Site plan.
(p.175, top left) Diagram:
figure and ground.
(p.175, top right) Diagram:
circulation.
(p.176-177) View of the
facades of three buildings from
the southwest.
Photos (pp.174-177) by
Bryan Nolan.
(below) Ground floor plan.
(opposite, bottom left and right)
Interior perspective views.

(p.174-175)南西から見た全景。
(p.174、下)配置図。
(p.175、左上)図と地。
(p.175、右上)動線。
(p.176-177)南西から見た三つの建物の
ファサード。
(下)1階平面図。
(次頁、下左右)内部を見る。

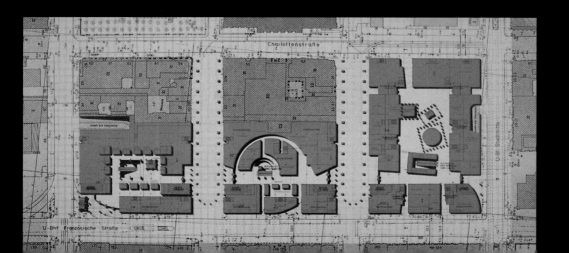

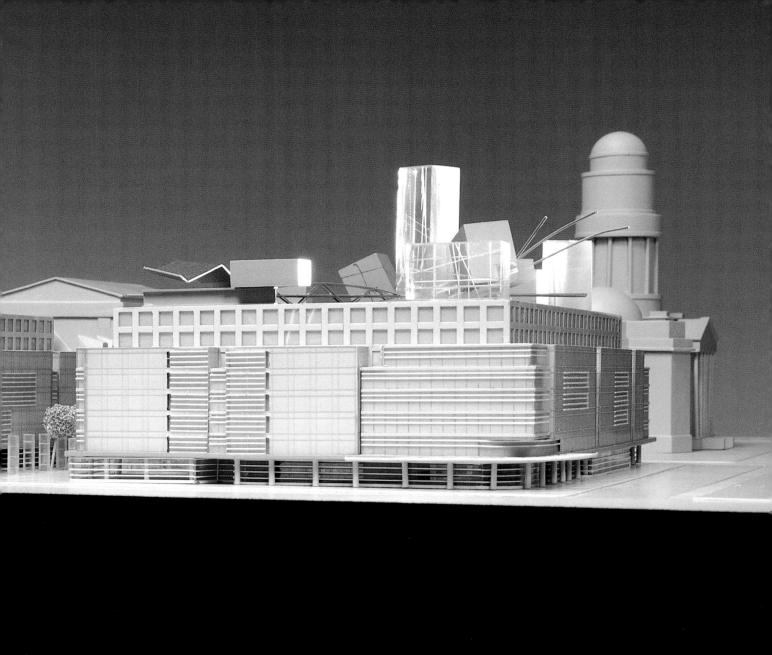

Hanseatic Trade Center

Hamburg, Germany

ハンザ同盟貿易センター
ドイツ、ハンブルク
1991

The design for the Hanseatic Trade Center located on the Elbe River, includes offices, a 250-room hotel, retail space, and the development of waterfront parks. In its organization, massing, and materials, this project seeks to draw upon images of Hamburg's harbor traditions, while also looking forward to its future position as a center for newly established East/West relations.

The proposed buildings on the site are of three types: (1) linear courtyard buildings continuing the massing of adjacent warehouses; (2) buildings developed as a series of pavilions; and, (3) object buildings forming the termination of the linear buildings. The use of brick reinforces the strong character of the adjacent masonry warehouses. The taller hotel structure, expressed as a glass and metal element relates to the industrial nature of the working harbor, while also serving as an illuminated beacon sparkling in the sunlight and radiating at night. Furthering the sense of symbolism, the hotel is designed to rise from a brick base, creating an icon rooted in the masonry of the past and soaring into the sky with a vision to the future.

エルベ川に位置するハンザ同盟貿易センターは、オフィスや250室のホテル、商業スペース、そしてウォーターフロントの公園の開発が一体となったものである。このプロジェクトは、その機構、構成、素材の扱い方においてハンブルク港の伝統的イメージを引きだそうと試みる一方、東西関係にとっての新しい中心としてのハンブルクの未来の役割を期待して表現したものでもある。提案された建物のタイプは三つである。

（1）隣接した倉庫群と軸を並べる中庭型の直線上の建物、（2）一連のパヴィリオン、そして（3）直線上の建物の端部に位置する、視線の焦点となる建物である。煉瓦を使用することは、近接する石造の倉庫街の堅固なキャラクターをさらに増すものである。また、高層のホテル棟は、ガラスと金属の建物として表現され、工業港としてのハンブルクのありのままの姿を表しながらさらに、あたかも灯台のごとく陽光の中でまたたき、闇夜に光を発するのである。シンボリズムの観念をつきつめた結果、ホテル棟は煉瓦の基壇から立ち上がることにより、石造建築に根ざす「過去」のイコンを形づくり、「未来」への指針をもちながら、空にそびえ立つのである。

（高木義雄訳）

(pp.178-179) View from the west.
Photo by Heiner Leiska.
(opposite, top) Elevations.
(opposite, bottom) Floor plan.

（p.178-179）西側から見た全景。
（次頁、上）立面図。
（次頁、下）平面図。

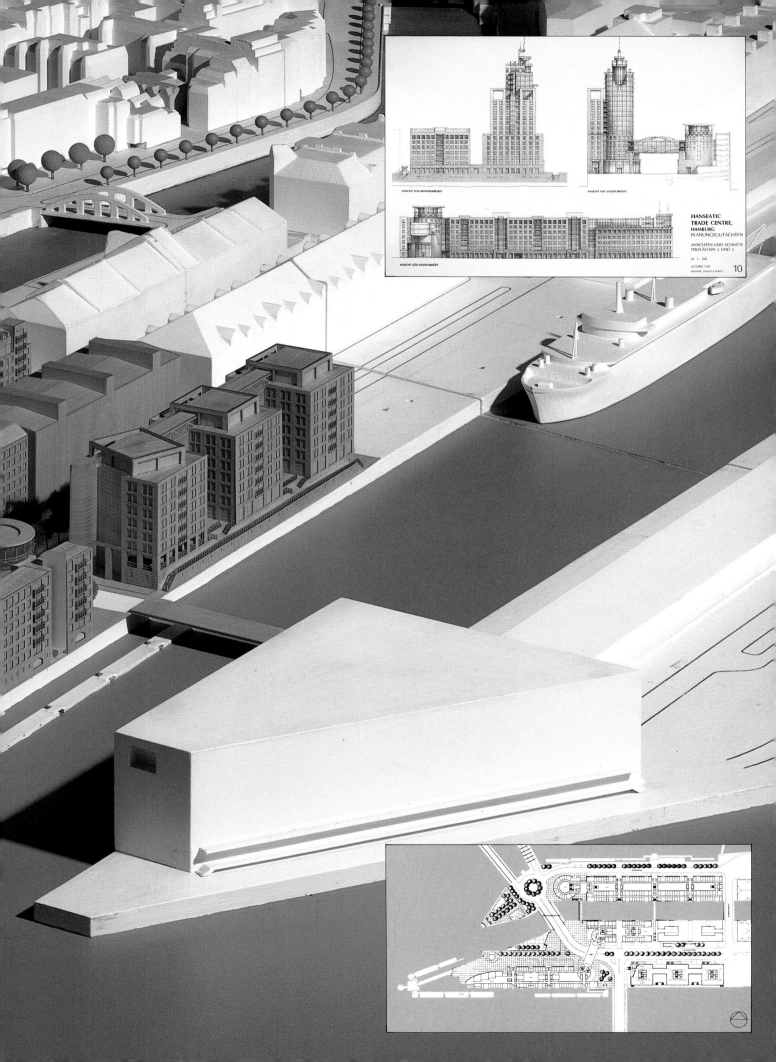

HANSEATIC
TRADE CENTRE,
HAMBURG
PLANUNGSGUTACHTEN

ANSICHTEN UND SCHNITTE
TEILFLÄCHEN 2 UND 3

M 1 : 200

OCTOBER 1990

10

ANSICHT SÜD-KEHRWIEDERFLEET

ANSICHT OST-SANDTORHÖFT

ANSICHT SÜD-SANDTORHÖFT

Federal Triangle

Washington, DC
in collaboration with Hammond Beeby and Babka, and Devrouax & Purnell

フェデラル・トライアングル
ワシントンDC

1989

The last major piece of land to be developed in the Federal Triangle
serves as the site for this project. The Federal Triangle is located at
the center of the nation's Capital, functioning as both a downtown
destination and a link between the tourist activities of the
Washington Mall and the city's rejuvenating downtown north of
Pennsylvania Avenue. In keeping with the Federal Triangle
Development Act passed by Congress in August 1987, the design of
the complex responds to the curves and masses of the grand classical
style of the Federal Triangle with a counterpoint of a rotunda topped
with a low, Jeffersonian dome and long splayed wings framing a
great plaza, fostering a dynamic interplay of old and new. The
program for the project includes 1,360,000 square feet of office
space for the nation's regulatory and administrative agencies,
500,000 square feet of exhibit space for the International Cultural
and Trade Center, space for restaurants and specialty retail, and four
levels of below-grade parking for 2,320 cars.

In addition to the collaborating architects, several architectural
offices contributed to this project including those of Michael Dennis,
Frank Gehry, Allan Greenberg, Patrick Pinnell, Elizabeth Plater-
Zyberk, and Adrian Smith.

このプロジェクトの敷地として、フェデラル・トライアングルの最後の開発区
域の大部分が提供された。フェデラル・トライアングルは、首都ワシントンの
中心部に位置する都心の目印であり、ワシントン・モールやペンシルヴェニア・
アヴェニューの北の活気づいた街をゆく旅行者の集まる場所として知られる。
1987年8月の議会でフェデラル・トライアングル開発計画が可決されたのにと
もなってデザインが開始された。低いジェファーソン・ドームと大きな広場を
囲む扇状に開いた長い翼をもつロトンダを対峙させる形で、フェデラル・トラ
イアングルの広大で伝統的なスタイルの曲線とマスに対応し、新旧のダイナミ
ックな干渉作用を引き起こしている。国の司法機関あるいは行政機関のための
12万6,000m²余のスペース、国際文化交流センターの展示に用いる4万6,000m²
のスペース、そしてレストランと専門店と、4層分の2,320台収容の駐車場を含
んでいる。

（河野裕訳）

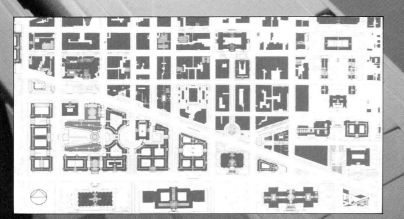

(pp.180-181) View from the
northwest.
Photo by Hoachlander
Photography associates.
(left) Site plan.
(opposite, top right) Selected
details.
(opposite, middle right) 14th
Street elevation.
(opposite, bottom right) Ground
floor plan.

（p.180-181）北西から見る。
（左）配置図。
（次頁、右上）ディテール。
（次頁、右中）14丁目側立面図。
（次頁、右下）1階平面図。

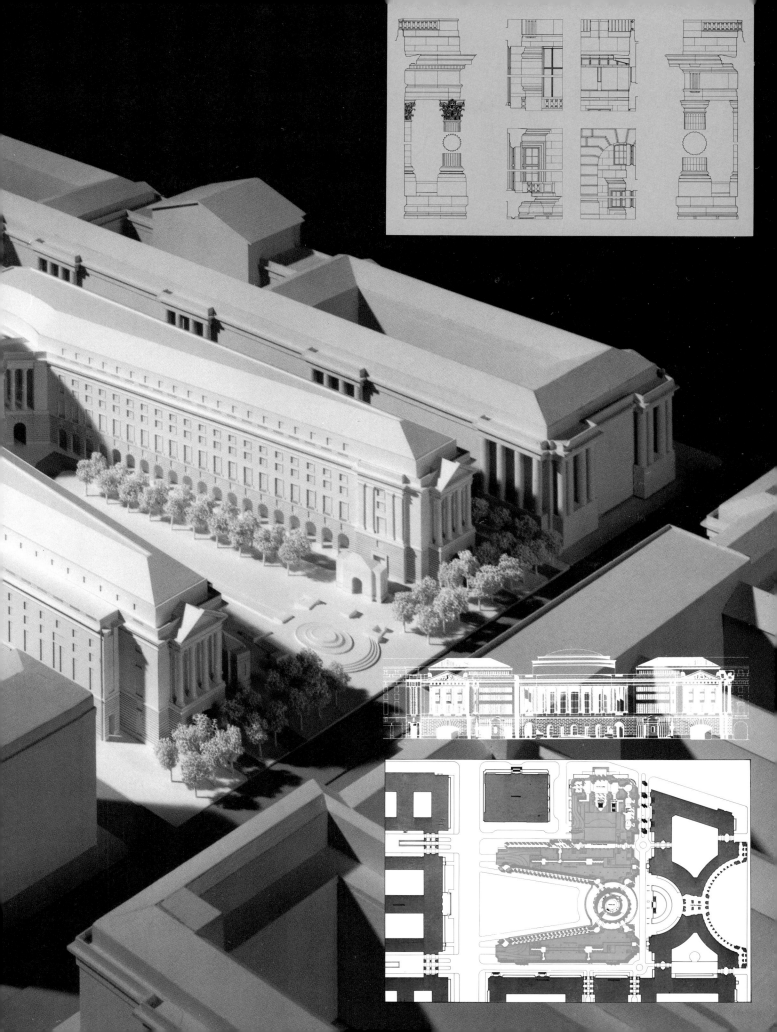

West Ferry Circus

Canary Wharf, London, England
in collaboration with Frank O. Gehry & Associates
キャナリィ・ワーフ・ウェスト・フェリィ・サーカス
英国、ロンドン
（フランク・ゲーリィとの共同設計）
1988

West Ferry Circus is the major point of entry to the 12-million-square-foot Canary Wharf development on the Isle of Dogs in the London Docklands. The design is a study of how to introduce a mix of residential and commercial uses of varying scales as a complement to the larger heart of Canary Wharf.
The plan, for which designs of individual elements were contributed by Stanley Tigerman, Thom Mayne and Michael Rotondi of Morphosis, and Tom Beeby, offers a dynamic interplay among building forms and open spaces. It emphasizes the relationship of Canary Wharf and West Ferry Circus to the Thames River, and welcomes those arriving by water from the City of London.

ウェスト・フェリィ・サーカスはロンドンの港湾地帯に浮かぶドッグス島にある。111万5,000㎡に渡って広がるキャナリィ・ワーフ開発の主玄関にあたる。このデザインは巨大なキャナリィ・ワーフに、いかにして様々なスケールの住宅や商業施設の複合体を付随させていくか、というスタディである。
この計画における個々の要素はスタンレィ・タイガーマン、モーフォシスのトム・メインとマイケル・ロトンディ、そしてトーマス・ビービィにより提案されたものである。要素の集合体としてのこの計画は、建築形態やオープン・スペースにダイナミックな相互作用を与え、かつテムズ川にたいするキャナリィ・ワーフとウェスト・フェリィ・サーカスの連携を強調する。そして、ロンドンのシティからの水路による来訪者を歓迎するのである。　　　（高木義雄訳）

(pp.182-183) View from above the gate bridge on the east to West Ferry Circus.
Photo by Monica Steve
(below) Site plan.
(opposite, top right) Elevation study.

（p.182-183）ウェスト・フェリィ・サーカスに入る東側のゲート・ブリッジ上方から見る。
モニカ・スティーブ撮影。
（次頁、右上）エレヴェーション・スタディ。

Carnegie Mellon University

Pittsburgh, Pennsylvania

カーネギー・メロン大学
ペンシルヴェニア州ピッツバーグ

1987

The Master Plan for Carnegie Mellon University began with the creation of an east/west axis for the campus, intersecting with the "Cut," a linear green space that extends from the university's main gate south to the library. At the northeast corner of the axis, a new 250-room student housing and dining facility complements an existing complex of dormitories across the street. West of the housing along the axis are indoor and outdoor student activity facilities that constitute the University Center. Adjacent to the center, a pool structure is vaulted over the axis, with glass end walls that allow views through to the 600-seat Perfoming Arts Theater beyond. Pavilions, which transform into lighted beacons at night, are strategically placed along the "Cut."

カーネギー・メロン大学のマスター・プランはキャンパスを横切る東西軸を設定することから始まった。この軸は大学の正門から南に、図書館まで延びる「カット」と呼ばれる緑地帯と交差する。

軸の東北部には、街路の向かい側の既存の寄宿舎に加えて、新たに250室の学生寮と食堂とを設置した。学生寮の西には東西軸に沿って、様々な学生のための施設が配置され、ユニヴァーシティ・センターを形成する。このセンターに隣接した軸上にはプールが配され、その上部にはヴォールト状の屋根が架かる。プールの端部の壁は透明なガラスとし、軸に沿ってプール越しに600人収容の芸術劇場が見通せるようにしている。また「カット」沿いにはいくつかのパヴィリオンを配した。夜にはパヴィリオンが灯台に一変する。　　(高木義雄訳)

(pp. 184-185) View of the natatorium along the Cut. (opposite, bottom left) Site plan. (top right) View of the Performing Arts Theater and the natatorium on the east/west axis from the east. Photo by Hoachlander Photography Associates.

(p.184-185)カット沿いの室内プールを見る。
(前頁、左下)配置図。
(右上)東西軸上の舞台芸術センター、室内プールを東側から見る。

Brooklyn Museum

Brooklyn, New York

ブルックリン美術館
ニューヨーク州ニューヨーク、ブルックリン

1986

The design concept for the expansion and renovation of the Brooklyn Museum responds to the intentions of the original design by McKim, Mead and White, while extending the monumental character of this historic and cultural landmark. The plan is based on axial and cross-axial relationships among museum and garden elements. The setting, garden, museum, and activity are integrated through a series of carefully conceived circulation paths and an architecturally ordered sequence of spaces, which become the central organizing spine for the old and new facilities. The building is centered around an exterior rectangular court that divides the museum into east and west wings and brings the landscape through the building to the Entrance Pavilion. Monumental stairs are reintroduced to reestablish visually the importance of the *piano nobile*. The new design is distinguished from the original museum through its use and detailing of materials.

ブルックリン美術館の拡張・修復におけるデザイン・コンセプトは、マッキム、ミード・アンド・ホワイトによるオリジナル・デザインの意図に応えるものであり、この歴史的・文化的意義をもった建物の記念碑的な性質を再評価しようというものである。平面計画は、美術館と庭園の間に介在する縦軸方向と横軸方向の関係をもとにしている。注意深く考えられた動線と、建築的に秩序だてられた空間の配列から成る一種の系が、新旧様々の機能を結ぶ背骨となった中央に組織され、背景、庭園、美術館、活動といったものをすべて、その中に統合している。建物は中央部の矩形の外庭を囲む形で集約されている。この庭により建物は東西の2棟に分けられており、エントランス・パヴィリオンへとランドスケープが建物を通り抜けて展開されている。モニュメンタルな階段を改めて取り入れることによって、ピアノ・ノービレ(主階)の佳重さを視覚的につなげている。

この新設計計画は、素材の使用や細部の扱い方によってもとの美術館とはっきり区別される。

(河野裕訳)

(p. 184) View from the
west
Photo by Nathaniel Lieberman
(top) Interior plan;
(right) perspective view
development with
window

Biography of David M. Childs

デイヴィッド・M・チャイルズ　略歴

David M. Childs, FAIA is Chairman of SOM and a Design Partner in the firm's New York office.

A graduate of Yale University, David Childs joined the Washington, D.C. office of SOM in 1971 after serving as Director of the Pennsylvania Avenue Commission, where he led the effort to prepare plans for the upgrading of the Nation's main ceremonial street. In 1975 he was appointed by the President to serve as Chairman of the National Capital Planning Commission, a position he filled from 1975 to 1981. His other civic involvements currently include membership on the boards of the American Academy in Rome, the Municipal Art Society, and the Architectural League. He is a Fellow of the American Institute of Architects.

Throughout his years of practice in Washington, David Childs became noted for his design of "appropriate architecture," buildings and spaces which respond to their settings and programs rather than pursue a preconceived architectural image. His projects in Washington include: the Bicentennial Landscaping of the Great Mall; Constitution Gardens; the National Geographic Society Headquarters; the U.S. News and World Report Headquarters; the Regent Hotel; the Evening Star Building; the new International Arrivals Building at Dulles International Airport, and numerous other public and private commissions.

In 1984, David Childs moved to SOM's New York office, applying his philosophy of "appropriateness" to a diverse range of projects in New York City including Worldwide Plaza on Eighth Avenue between 49th and 50th Streets; the Master Plan for Riverside South; One Broadway Place, a retail-and-office project on Times Square at 45th Street; 450 Lexington Avenue, an office tower above the Grand Central Post Office; and Columbus Center, a 2.6-million-square-foot mixed-use complex to rise at Columbus Circle in Central Park.

Domestically, David Childs is presently working on a wide range of projects in New York City; the new Federal Courthouse in Charleston, West Virginia; the regional headquarters for the FBI in Washington, D.C.; and the Sallie Mae office complex in Herndon, Virginia. His current international work includes a hotel in Brussels; two office towers in São Paulo; a mixed-use, full-block project at Checkpoint Charlie in Berlin; the American Embassy in Ottawa; and a major urban redevelopment in Mexico City.

In addition, David Childs has often been a juror on local and national design award programs, a design critic at a variety of professional schools, and a lecturer and panelist at numerous conferences and symposia. His work has been widely published in the architectural press.

デイヴィッド・M・チャイルズは、SOMの会長であり、SOMニューヨーク事務所のデザイン・パートナーでもある。

イェール大学を卒業し、ワシントンのペンシルヴェニア・アヴェニュー委員会理事の職についた。この委員会で、彼は合衆国の中枢となるこの通りをさらに整備するための計画に力をつくしたのち、1971年に、SOMワシントンDC事務所に入った。1975年、首都計画委員会の議長に大統領から任命され、1981年までつとめた。現在、彼が理事・委員として関わっているこういった公的な活動に、ローマのアメリカン・アカデミィ、ニューヨーク市芸術協会、建築連盟などがある。もちろんAIA（アメリカ建築家協会）の会員でもある。

ワシントンでの仕事をとおして、チャイルズは、予見的な建築像を追求するというよりは、建築や空間をその社会背景や環境、そしてプログラムに応じてつくりあげる「適合建築」をデザインするということでよく知られるようになった。ワシントンで彼が手がけた仕事には、ワシントン・モール200年記念修景計画、コンスティテューション庭園、米国地理学協会本部ビル、USニューズ・レポート本社、リージェント・ホテル、イヴニング・スター・ビル、ダレス空港国際線到着ビル新棟など、数多くの公共および民間の計画がある。

1984年、デイヴィッド・チャイルズはSOMニューヨーク事務所に移った。彼は、ニューヨークでの多種多様な計画に「適合」という彼の哲学をもってした。そういった作品に、8番街のワールドワイド・プラザ、リヴァーサイド・サウス・マスター・プラン、ワン・ブロードウェイ・プレイス、450レキシントン・アヴェニュー、コロンバス・センターなどがある。

現在、デイヴィッド・チャイルズは、国内においては、ニューヨーク・シティでの広範なプロジェクト、ウェストヴァージニア州チャールストンの連邦裁判所、ワシントンDCのFBI地方本庁、ヴァージニア州ハーンドンのサリー・メイ・オフィス・コンプレックスなどのプロジェクトについている。

また国外での仕事には、ブリュッセルのホテル、サンパウロでの二つのオフィス・タワー、ベルリンのチェックポイント・チャーリーの多目的ビル、オタワのアメリカ大使館、そしてメキシコ・シティでの大規模な都市再開発計画などがある。

デイヴィッド・チャイルズは、地域規模の、また全国規模のデザイン賞の審査員、建築学部のデザイン批評、講演会やシンポジウムの講師およびパネリストといった仕事にも携わっている。

彼の仕事は広く建築関係の出版物に紹介されている。

Photo of D.M.Childs by Bachrach, and photo at the back by Addison Thompson.

Biographies of Contributors

寄稿者略歴

Richard Sennett

Richard Sennett, who conducted the interview with David Childs presented in this issue, is a writer about urban culture and social thought, and is also a novelist. He writes for scholarly journals and also for *The New York Review of Books, The Times Literary Supplement, The New Yorker, Partisan Review*, and other periodicals, and has authored more than a dozen books.

Richard Sennett received a B.A., 1964, in history, with special honors, from the University of Chicago, and a Ph. D., 1969, from Harvard University, Committee on Higher Degrees in American Civilization.

Richard Sennett is the founder of two institutes: the Cambridge Institute, Cambridge, Massachusetts, a research and policy analysis center; and the New York Institute for the Humanities, located at New York University. Currently he chairs the Committee on Urban Studies, sponsored by UNESCO. The Committee seeks to relate architecture and urban design to the social sciences.

Richard Sennett serves as an advisor to the International Social Science Council, and as advisor in sociology to the National Science Foundation. In New York, he is a member of the Committee for New York, a citizens group organized under the auspices of the Municipal Art Society to monitor issues of public concern in the city.

Paul Goldberger

Paul Goldberger, author of "David Childs" published in this issue, is Cultural News Editor of *The New York Times*. He continues to serve as the architecture critic of *The New York Times*, a position he has held since 1973. He has also written books on architecture, including *The City Observed—New York: An Architectural Guide to Manhattan* (Random House/Vintage Books), *The Skyscraper* (Alfred Knopf), and *Above New York* (Cameron Books).

He was born in Nutley, New Jersey, and educated at Yale University, where he received a Bachelor of Arts degree in the history of art. He joined *The New York Times Sunday Magazine* staff in 1972, and moved to the daily paper as architecture critic in 1973.

Since 1984, Paul Goldberger has been Visiting Lecturer at the Yale School of Architecture, where he teaches a course in architecture criticism.

Paul Goldberger's architectural criticism has been honored with awards, including the Pulitzer Prize for Distinguished Criticism, the highest award in journalism, in recognition of his architecture writings in the *Times* (1984), and the medal of the American Institute of Architects (1981).

Marilyn Jordan Taylor

Marilyn Jordan Taylor, who wrote "Six Projects for New York City," is the partner responsible for urban design and planning in SOM's East Coast office. In this role, she has worked closely with David Childs on the projects presented in this issue.

Since joining SOM in 1971, Marilyn J. Taylor's work has also included numerous transportation projects, including the stations program of the Northeast Corridor Passenger Rail Improvement Project, the expansion of Dulles International Airport, and the design standards for the growth of Logan Airport in Boston, Massachusetts. Active in the community, she is a board member of the New York City AIA, the Institute for Urban Design, the Regional and Urban Design Committee of the AIA, the Buell Center for American Architecture, and the New York City Building Congress.

リチャード・セネット

リチャード・セネットは、都市文化や社会思想について執筆する一方、小説も書いている。それらは学術団体の会誌や『ニューヨーク・レヴュー・オヴ・ブックス』『ザ・タイムズ文芸増刊号』『ザ・ニューヨーカー』『パルティザン・レヴュー』など多数の雑誌に発表されている。また10冊を越す著作を著している。

セネットは、1964年にシカゴ大学において史学の学士号を首席で得、1969年、ハーヴァード大学よりアメリカ文明の研究にたいして博士号を授けられた。

彼は、マサチューセッツ州ケンブリッジに学術研究と政策分析センターであるケンブリッジ研究所を、またニューヨーク大学におかれたニューヨーク人文科学研究所を設立した。現在セネットは、UNESCO後援による都市研究委員会の議長をつとめている。この委員会は社会科学と建築・都市デザインとの関わりを探求している。また彼は、国際社会科学会議、および国立科学財団の社会学の部門でのアドヴァイザーもつとめている。さらにセネットは、ニューヨークの公益に関する諸問題を検討するために、市芸術協会の後援により組織された市民団体であるニューヨーク委員会のメンバーでもある。

ポール・ゴールドバーガー

ポール・ゴールドバーガーは、『ニューヨーク・タイムズ』紙の文化欄の編集長である。彼は、1973年以来同紙の建築批評を担当している。建築に関する著作、『都市を見る—ニューヨーク：マンハッタン建築ガイド』(ランダム・ハウス社、ヴィンテージ・ブックス)、『摩天楼』(アルフレッド・ノフ社)、『ニューヨークの上に』(キャメロン・ブックス社) なども著している。

ポール・ゴールドバーガーはニュージャージィ州ナトリィに生まれた。イェール大学に学び、美術史において学士号を得た。1972年に『ニューヨーク・タイムズ・サンディ・マガジン』のスタッフとなり、1973年にその日刊紙の建築批評を受けもつことになったのである。

1984年にイェールの建築学部の客員講師となり、以来今も「建築批評」の講座を担当している。彼の建築批評は高く評価され、1981年に、AIAよりメダルを、1984年には、『タイムズ』での建築批評が認められ、ジャーナリズムで最高のピューリッツァー賞を授けられた。

マリリン・ジョーダン・テイラー

本書で「ニューヨーク・シティ、6プロジェクト」を執筆しているマリリン・J・テイラーは、SOMイースト・コースト事務所の都市計画部門の責任担当のパートナーである。この立場から彼女はこの本に掲載されているプロジェクトをデイヴィッド・チャイルズとともに取り組んだ。

1971年にSOMに入った彼女は、数多くの交通施設計画に取り組んだ。北東地域旅客鉄道線改良計画、ダレス国際空港増築計画、ボストンのローガン空港拡張基準計画などがある。建築界での活動として、AIAニューヨーク・シティ、都市計画協会、AIA地域・都市計画委員会、アメリカ建築のためのビューエル・センター、さらにニューヨーク・シティ建設委員会などの委員を引き受けている。